Encyclopedia of CREATIVE COOKING

Volume 1
Soups & Starters

Editors for U.S. editions
Steve Sherman and Julia Older

ECB Enterprises Inc.

Soups

Clear soups, like consommé, are light on the palate and ideal for formal dinner parties. Hearty soups— broths, purées and brews packed with chunks of meat, fish, rice, pasta or vegetables—can easily be meals in themselves. Creamy soups, thickened by the addition of cream, egg yolk or flour, demand greater care in their making

Stocks

A full-bodied flavorsome stock is the basis of so many good dishes but especially of soups — even packet and canned soups can be pepped up and enriched by stock — sauces, gravies and many casserole dishes.

Most of us use ready-made stock preparations like the cubes just to save time, but they are often highly seasoned and very salty, so exercise care when adding seasonings. But if you take the trouble to make your own stock, you'll get a lot more satisfaction from a dish — and a tastier one as well.

There's an economic stock, largely using whatever is on hand, a white or chicken base for light-colored soups and sauces, a brown base for consommé, dark soups, sauces and gravy, and a fish base.

A really concentrated bone stock sets as a firm gelatin when cold, and slow and lengthy cooking is the only way to concentrate the flavors.

Unlike soups to which almost anything can be added, stock must be clear — vital when making consomme or aspic (savory gelatin) — so avoid using starchy foods like rice and potatoes, or thickened liquids, which will turn it cloudy; and leave out strongly-flavored vegetables like turnip and cabbage, as well as mutton bones, which will give a bitter taste.

Make as large a pan of stock as possible (a pressure cooker will save time and fuel) and, if not using at once, keep stock in the refrigerator for a couple of days — otherwise boil up daily. Fish stock, however, should always be used the same day.

Household Stock

2 lbs. raw or cooked beef bones
1 onion
1 carrot
1 branch celery (optional)
8½ cups cold water
1 bouquet garni
1 teaspoon salt
6 peppercorns

1 Wash the bones. Peel, wash and roughly chop the onion and carrot; wash and chop the celery.

2 Put the bones in a large stewpan, add the water, bring to a boil and remove any scum that rises to the surface.

3 Add the chopped vegetables, bouquet garni and seasonings to the pan. Reduce the heat and simmer, with the pan lid on, for about 4 hours.

4 Strain the stock and then let cool. When cold remove the fat from the surface.

Makes about 6¼ cups

Tip: additions to this stock can include tomato paste, meat trimmings and leftovers (but not liver), bacon rinds and cooked ham bones.

Brown Stock

2 lbs. raw beef marrow bones or knuckle of veal bones
1 lb. lean stewing beef
2 onions
2 carrots
1 branch celery
8½ cups cold water
1 bouquet garni
1 teaspoon salt
6 peppercorns

1 Wash the bones and meat and dry on absorbent paper. Cut the meat into about 1-inch cubes.

2 Peel, wash and chop the onions and carrots; wash and chop the celery.

3 Put the chopped bones, cubes of beef and the chopped onion in a roasting pan and bake in a moderate oven 350°F. until well browned.

4 Strain off any fat in the pan, then transfer the bones, beef and onion to a large stewpan. Add the water, sliced carrots and celery, bouquet garni and seasonings. Bring to a boil, remove any scum, reduce the heat, cover the pan, and simmer 5 hours.

5 Strain the stock and then let cool. When cold remove the fat from the surface

Makes about 6¼ cups.

White Stock

2 lbs. raw knuckle of veal, (chopped), or stewing veal
10 cups cold water
½ teaspoon lemon juice
1 onion
1 carrot
1 bouquet garni
1 teaspoon salt
6 peppercorns

1 Wash the veal bones, then put them in a large stewpan with the water and lemon juice. Bring to a boil and skim off any scum that rises to the surface.

2 Meanwhile, peel, wash and slice the onion and carrot.

3 Add the sliced vegetables, bouquet garni, salt and peppercorns to the pan of bones, bring back to a boil, then reduce the heat and simmer, with the lid on, for about 5 hours.

4 Strain the stock and then let cool. When cold remove the fat from the surface.

Makes about 6¼ cups

Chicken Stock

1-2 raw or cooked chicken carcasses and bones
$\frac{1}{2}$ lb. chicken giblets, excluding the
  liver
$8\frac{1}{2}$ cups cold water
2 onions
2 carrots
1 bouquet garni
1 teaspoon salt
6 peppercorns

1 Wash the chicken carcasses, bones and giblets. Put them in a large stewpan, add the water, bring to a boil and remove any scum that rises to the surface.

2 Meanwhile, peel, wash and slice the onions and carrots.

3 Add the sliced vegetables and seasonings to the pan, bring back to a boil, then reduce the heat and simmer, with the lid on, for about 3 hours.

4 Strain the stock and then let cool. When cold remove the fat from the surface.

Makes about $6\frac{1}{4}$ cups

Variation: to make turkey or game stock, substitute the appropriate carcasses, giblets and feet, if used, for the chicken ingredients.

Fish Stock

2 lbs. fresh fish heads, or fish
  bones and trimmings
1 carrot (optional)
1 onion
6 cups cold water, or half water
  and half dry white wine
1 teaspoon salt
4 peppercorns
1 bouquet garni

1 Wash the fish heads or bones and trimmings well. Peel and cut up the carrot, if used, and the onion.

2 Put the fish pieces in a large pan, add the water, bring to a boil and skim the surface. Add the vegetables, salt, peppercorns and bouquet garni to the pan, bring back to a boil and cover. Reduce the heat and simmer slowly for about 40 minutes when the stock should be reduced.

3 Strain the stock through clean cheesecloth or a fine strainer, cover and cool; refrigerate until required.

Makes about $4\frac{1}{2}$ cups

Tip: fish stock should always be used the same day it is made.

Stock, other than fish, can be frozen up to 6 months. Strain it, cool and skim off any fat. Boiling stock down to one-third its volume concentrates it, and it can then be frozen as single cubes in ice trays and diluted with water for use.

Bouquet Garni

Many recipes call for the use of a bouquet garni, the French name for a small bunch of herbs, either fresh or dried, which is used to flavor dishes. The traditional bouquet garni is made up of a bay leaf, a sprig or two of parsley and thyme, and a few peppercorns, all tied in a small piece of cheesecloth.

It doesn't matter too much which herbs are used so long as they are aromatic, so you can experiment with different mixtures, incorporating herbs like chervil, basil, rosemary and tarragon.

Ready-made bouquet garnis in cheesecloth or paper sachets are available, but the paper ones tend to disintegrate with long cooking.

Hearty Soups

Mulligatawny

Created in the days of the British in India, this soup is basically a rich meat stock flavored with curry, and can be made with any meat.

1 lb. lean breast of lamb
1 large onion
1 medium carrot
1 small green tart apple
2 tablespoons oil
1 tablespoon curry powder
salt and pepper
2 tablespoons flour
6 cups brown stock
$\frac{3}{4}$ cup milk
1 teaspoon cornstarch
1 tablespoon cold water
1 teaspoon lemon juice

1 Wipe and trim lamb of excess fat; cut into $\frac{1}{2}$-inch wide strips. Peel and slice the onion and carrot; peel, core and slice the apple.

2 Heat the oil in a large pan. When hot, brown the lamb all over. Take out and add the sliced vegetables and apple and cook, stirring, for about 5 minutes. Stir in the curry powder and cook for a further 2 minutes, then blend in the flour. Add the stock, bring to a boil and return the meat to the pan. Cover and simmer gently for about $1\frac{1}{2}$ hours.

3 Take out the meat and any bones. Rub the liquid through a strainer or purée in a blender. Return the purée to a clean pan. Stir in the milk and reheat but do not boil. Blend the cornstarch with the cold water, stir into the soup and heat nearly to boiling point till thick. Check the seasoning and serve.

Serves 6

Beef and Carrot Soup

1 small onion
1 lb. carrots
1 medium potato
3 tablespoons butter
½ teaspoon salt
freshly ground black pepper
½ teaspoon sugar
3 cups brown stock
1 tablespoon chopped parsley
1 teaspoon chopped chervil or
  marjoram

1 Peel and chop the onion; peel and dice the carrots and potato.

2 Melt the butter in a heavy saucepan and add the carrots, onion and potato. Add the salt, pepper and sugar. Cover the pan and cook over low heat for 15 minutes.

3 Add the stock and bring to a boil. Lower the heat, cover the pan and cook for a further 15 minutes. Rub the soup through a strainer or purée in a blender.

4 Reheat until hot, then serve, sprinkling on the chopped herbs.

Serves 4

Fresh Pea Soup

1 head (Boston) lettuce
½ cup butter
1 lb. shelled fresh peas
½ teaspoon salt
1 teaspoon sugar
4 cups chicken stock
freshly ground black pepper

1 Wash the lettuce, drain well, tear the leaves into pieces.

2 Heat the butter in a saucepan, add the lettuce pieces, shelled peas, salt and sugar. Cover the pan, reduce the heat and let the vegetables cook gently over low heat for about 10 minutes. Stir in the stock,

cover and simmer 10 minutes more or until the peas are tender.

3 Purée the soup by rubbing through a strainer or purée in a blender. Return the pea purée to a clean saucepan, add black pepper to taste and heat again until just simmering. Serve at once.

Serves 4

Minestrone

1 carrot
4 potatoes
1 small white cabbage
½ bunch celery
1 cup shelled fresh peas
5 tomatoes
1 clove garlic
4 slices bacon
2 onions
2 tablespoons oil
8½ cups white or brown stock
2-3 tablespoons chopped mixed
  herbs
salt and pepper
¼ cup macaroni
grated Parmesan cheese

1 Peel and dice the carrots and potatoes; trim and cut up the cabbage and celery in small pieces. Wash them well. Skin the tomatoes, then cut them in half and scoop out the seeds. Cut the tomato pulp into small cubes. Peel and crush the garlic. Cut the bacon into strips. Peel and chop the onions.

2 Heat the oil in a large pan and when hot sauté the bacon, onion, carrots, cabbage, celery and tomatoes. Add the stock with the crushed garlic, chopped mixed herbs and salt and pepper to taste. Cover and cook for 1 hour over low heat. Then add the diced potato and the peas and continue cooking for a further 15 minutes.

3 During this time, cook the macaroni in a pan of boiling salted water for about 15 minutes or until just tender. Drain and set aside.

4 When the soup is cooked, add the macaroni and serve immediately with grated Parmesan cheese separately.

Serves 6

Italian Egg Soup

Zuppa Pavese is the Italian name for this very nourishing soup. Instead of poaching the eggs in the stock as we do here, the eggs may be broken into the individual bowls and the boiling stock then poured on. However, the eggs tend not to be cooked sufficiently this way. It is such a substantial soup that only a light main course should follow.

2 cups brown stock
2 cups chicken stock
4 slices sandwich bread
8 very fresh eggs
2 tablespoons oil
¼ cup grated Parmesan cheese
2 tablespoons chopped mixed
  herbs

1 Mix the 2 stocks together in a large pan and put over low heat. Cut the slices of bread into small cubes.

2 Break the eggs, one by one, into a saucer and slide them carefully down the side of the pan into the stock. Draw the white back onto the yolk with a fork to get neat, poached eggs.

3 While the eggs are poaching, heat the oil in a skillet and fry the cubes of bread in it. Then drain them.

4 Put 2 poached eggs into each soup bowl. Pour in the stock and divide the cubes of bread, the Parmesan and the mixed herbs between each; serve.

Serves 4

Minestrone is one of Italy's best known soups and easily a meal in itself. Regional variations are many, ranging from the addition of fresh basil and pork to substituting a goat's milk cheese for Parmesan

Look 'n Cook Farmhouse Soup

1 Ingredients: leeks, carrots, turnips, celery, peas, beans, bacon, potatoes, cabbage, butter 2 Peel the carrots and turnips, trim the leeks and dice 3 Soften the vegetables in the butter 4 Moisten with water or stock. Add the bacon and shredded cabbage; season with salt and pepper and bring to a boil 5 String and

chop the beans **6** Peel and dice the potatoes; place in a bowl of cold water to remove excess starch **7** Drain the potatoes, then add all the vegetables to the pan

8 Take out the bacon and dice; put in tureen **9** Serve the soup, with the croûtons and grated cheese separately

Farmhouse Soup

2 carrots
2 turnips
whites of 2 leeks
2 branches celery
½ green cabbage
¼ cup butter
1 lb. bacon, thickly sliced
9 cups white or chicken stock
salt and pepper
1¼ cups string beans
2 potatoes
1¼ cups shelled peas
¾ cup grated Gruyère cheese

1 Peel the carrots and turnips, and wash them. Wash the whites of the leeks and the celery. Cut them all into small cubes. Wash and cut the cabbage into thin strips.

2 Melt the butter in a large pan. Put in the prepared vegetables and soften on low heat for 10 minutes; stirring from time to time.

3 Wash the bacon in cold water, then put it into a saucepan. Cover with cold water, bring to a boil and simmer for 10 minutes on low heat. Then drain and rinse in cold water.

4 Add the stock to the vegetables, then add the bacon, cabbage and salt and pepper. Bring to a boil, then reduce the heat, cover and simmer very gently for about 1¼ hours.

5 Remove the 'strings' from the beans, wash them and cut into pieces about 1½ inches in length. Peel the potatoes. Wash and cut them into tiny cubes. Cover with water and let soak.

6 About 20 minutes before the end of the cooking time, drain the potatoes. Add them to the soup with the peas and the green beans. Leave to finish cooking.

7 Heat a soup tureen. Put the grated Gruyère cheese into a bowl. Drain the bacon, cut into cubes and put into the tureen. Pour on the rest

of the soup. Serve the soup with croûtons and the Gruyère cheese served separately.

Serves 4

Rose-colored Cauliflower Soup

1 small cauliflower
3 potatoes
small bunch of chervil
5½ cups salted water
2 tablespoons tomato paste
salt and pepper
4 tablespoons rice flour
2¼ cups milk
2 tablespoons butter

1 Wash the cauliflower and divide it into small florets. Peel and dice the potatoes.

2 Bring the salted water to a boil. Add the cauliflower and diced potatoes to the water and boil gently for 30 minutes. Cool a little, then rub through a strainer or purée in a blender.

3 Return the purée to the pan and heat, mixing in the tomato paste and seasoning with salt and pepper.

4 Mix the rice flour to a smooth paste with a little of the milk and then mix in the rest. Add to the soup. Cook for 10 minutes more over low heat, stirring constantly. Wash, dry and chop the chervil.

5 Put the butter in a heated tureen, pour on the soup, sprinkle on the chervil and serve.

Serves 6

Rose-colored Cauliflower Soup

Belgian Leek Soup

3 tablespoons butter
½ lb. leeks, or 4 onions
1 lb. potatoes
6 cups beef stock
1 teaspoon salt

Belgian Leek Soup — nourishing and one of the simplest soups

½ cup light cream or milk
4-6 slices toasted French bread

1 Trim and wash the leeks well, then slice or peel and slice the onions. Peel and dice the potatoes.

2 Heat the butter in a large pan, add the prepared leeks or onions, and sauté gently for 3 minutes. Add the diced potatoes, beef stock and salt, and bring to a boil. Cover with a lid, reduce the heat and simmer for 40 minutes, stirring occasionally.

3 When ready to serve, stir in the cream or milk. Place a slice of toasted bread in each soup bowl and pour on the hot soup.

Serves 4–6

Look 'n Cook French Onion Soup

1 Ingredients: onions, butter, flour, stock, wine, bread, eggs, cheese, salt and pepper **2** Peel and chop onions **3** Brown onions in half the butter **4** Stir in the flour till it browns **5** Add liquid, garlic, salt and pepper, then simmer **6** Toast the slices of bread **7** Poach the eggs and set aside in a bowl of warm water

till required **8** When the soup is cooked, divide among individual flameproof bowls **9** Place a poached egg in each soup bowl **10** Butter the toasted slices of bread and sprinkle with grated cheese **11** Put a slice of bread in each bowl **12** Brown the cheese under a hot broiler

Normandy Soup

giblets of 2 chickens
½ cup butter
salt and pepper
8½ cups white or chicken stock
1 small bouquet garni
½ lb. green beans
2 zucchini
4 small carrots
2 turnips
3 potatoes
1 small branch celery
white part of 2 leeks
1 onion
2 tomatoes
few lettuce leaves
1 cup light cream

1 Put the washed giblets into cold water, bring to a boil and drain. Heat 4 tablespoons butter in a stewpan and lightly fry the giblets in it. Add the salt, pepper, stock and bouquet garni. Bring to a boil, cover with the lid, reduce the heat and simmer for 20 minutes.

2 During this time, remove the 'strings' from the beans and cut them into small pieces. Peel the zucchini, the carrots, the turnips and the potatoes, and dice them. Wash the celery and chop it into tiny slices. Wash and slice the white part of the leeks. Peel and chop the onion.

3 Skin and quarter the tomatoes, remove seeds, then cut the pulp into small pieces. Wash and dry the lettuce and shred.

4 Melt the rest of the butter in a saucepan and cook all the vegetables in it until they begin to color. When the giblets have cooked for 20 minutes, add the vegetables to them and continue simmering for a further hour. Then heat the soup tureen.

5 Remove the bouquet garni. Put the cream into the hot tureen, whisk in the soup and serve.

Serves 6

Tip: During the winter months the green beans can be replaced by soaked, dried navy beans and the zucchini left out, or frozen vegetables can be used.

Portuguese Lobster Soup

2 large onions
2 large carrots
3 medium potatoes
3 cloves garlic
4 cups water
1 cup dry white wine
1 teaspoon salt
12 peppercorns
2-lb. live lobster
2 tablespoons oil
1 cup tomato paste
¾ cup long grain rice
1 tablespoon finely chopped
  parsley
½ teaspoon ground coriander
freshly ground pepper
2 tablespoons brandy

1 Peel and finely chop the onions and carrots; peel and dice the potatoes; peel and crush the garlic cloves.

2 Put the water, white wine, half the chopped onions and carrots, the potatoes, salt and peppercorns in a large saucepan and bring to a boil. Reduce the heat and simmer for 30 minutes. Then put in the lobster and simmer again for about 30 minutes or until the lobster is cooked.

3 Heat the oil in another large saucepan until hot; add the remaining chopped onions and carrots and fry until lightly browned. Stir in the tomato paste and take the pan off the heat.

4 Take out the cooked lobster, strain the cooking liquor and reserve. Split the lobster in half lengthwise, crack the claws and take out the meat from the tail shell and the claws; cut it into ½-inch pieces. Break the lobster shell into pieces (use either a hammer or nut crackers), put them into a pan with the reserved cooking liquor and simmer for 20 minutes.

5 Strain the liquor again and stir into the tomato mixture. Add the raw rice, parsley, coriander, pepper and garlic and simmer for 30 minutes. Stir in the lobster meat pieces and brandy and simmer for another 5 minutes. Check the seasoning and serve at once.

Serves 8–10

Traditional Meatball Soup

6 cups brown stock
¼ lb. ground beef
½ teaspoon salt
freshly ground pepper
3 tablespoons finely chopped
  parsley
2 tablespoons oil
1 teaspoon paprika
½ cup long grain rice
2 cloves garlic
3 tablespoons vinegar

1 Put the stock into a large pan and bring to simmering point. Mix the beef with the salt, pepper and 2 tablespoons of the chopped parsley. Form into small balls about 1 inch in diameter.

2 Add the meatballs to the stock and simmer 15 minutes.

3 Heat the oil in a small pan, stir in the paprika and cook for 2 minutes. Stir this into the soup.

4 Add the rice to the soup, cover the pan and simmer 15 minutes or until the rice is tender. Stir in the rest of the parsley, garlic and vinegar. Serve at once.

Serves 6

Normandy Soup—a hearty broth flavored with chicken

French Onion Soup

½ lb. onions
1 clove garlic
⅓ cup butter
2 tablespoons flour
3¼ cups stock
1 cup dry white wine
salt and pepper
4 large slices white bread
scant 1 cup grated cheese
¼ cup white vinegar
4 eggs

1 Peel and chop the onions. Peel and crush the garlic.

2 Melt half the butter in a sauté pan. Add the onions and cook them. When they are golden, add the flour and stir with a wooden spoon until the flour browns.

3 Add the stock and the wine, mixing in well. Add the crushed garlic. Cook for about 40 minutes. Adjust the seasoning without stinting on the pepper.

4 Meanwhile, cut the bread into rounds. Toast them or dry in a low oven.

5 Boil some water in a saucepan. Add the vinegar. Break the eggs one by one into a cup, put each carefully into the pan and let them poach just enough to allow them to be removed without breaking. Keep them warm in a dish containing warm water.

6 When the soup is ready, divide it among flameproof bowls.

7 Place a poached egg in each dish. Butter the slices of bread and sprinkle with grated cheese. Put a slice of bread in each bowl and brown quickly under a hot broiler (the eggs must not continue to cook). Serve piping hot.

Serves 4

Tip: This is a good dish for a small dinner party; if preferred, the poached eggs can be omitted from the soup.

Red Pepper and Tomato Soup

1 onion
2 medium red peppers
1 large tomato
1 large leek
4 tablespoons butter
1 tablespoon finely chopped parsley
4½ cups chicken stock
salt and pepper
¼ cup flour

1 Peel and chop the onion. Cut the red pepper in half, remove the seeds and white membrane and chop. Skin and cut the tomato in half, scoop out the seeds and chop the pulp roughly. Trim the outer leaves of the leek and cut off the root; cut in half, wash well, then slice thinly.

2 Heat half the butter in a large pan, put in the onions, red pepper and leek and cook gently until the onions are soft and translucent. Add the chopped tomato and parsley and cook for about 2 minutes.

3 Pour in the stock, add salt and pepper, bring to a boil, cover the pan, reduce the heat and simmer for about 15 minutes or until the vegetables are tender.

4 Soften the remaining butter and, using a fork, blend with the flour to make kneaded butter, then stir this into the soup. Bring to a boil, stirring until the soup thickens. Serve at once.

Serves 6

French Onion Soup

This classic country hotpot of meat and vegetables in broth hails from France where it is called pot-au-feu. *A two-in-one dish — serve the broth first, with toast, then follow with the beef and vegetables. Turn page for the recipe and step-by-step guide for Hotpot Soup plus a variation using four different meats*

Look 'n Cook Hotpot Soup

1 Tie the beef with string so it holds its shape during cooking **2** Put the beef and bones in a large pot with the water **3** Peel and quarter the carrots and turnips; halve the leeks and celery **4** Add the vegetables, bouquet garni and seasonings and cook **5** and **6** Wrap up the marrowbone, add to pot and cook

Hotpot Soup (Pot-au-fcu)

4½ lbs. stewing beef, in one piece
1-2 beef bones
13 cups water
1 bouquet garni
1½ lbs. carrots
1 lb. turnips
1½ lbs. leeks
1 bunch celery
2 large onions
2 cloves garlic
4 cloves
1 large marrowbone, about 4
   inches long

1 Tie the meat with thin string so it holds its shape during cooking. Place it in a large pot together with the beef bones. Add all the water except for ¼ cup and bring slowly to a boil with the lid off.

2 Meanwhile, if using fresh herbs for the bouquet garni, tie them together. Peel the onions and garlic; stud the onion with the cloves.

3 Peel and quarter the carrots lengthwise; peel and quarter the turnips. Trim and cut away the roots of the leeks, then cut in half and wash in several changes of water, fanning out the green stems, so all the dirt is removed. Trim the root end of the celery and discard the green leaves; then quarter and tie the pieces together with the leeks.

4 When the surface of the liquid is covered with scum, take the pot off the heat; pour in the reserved water and skim at once. Return the pot to the heat, cover with a lid and simmer slowly for 1 hour. Then add the prepared vegetables, bouquet garni, garlic, onions, salt and pepper, and cook slowly for a further 1¾ hours.

5 Wrap the marrowbone in cheese-cloth and tie with string; this will stop the marrow from slipping out of the bone. Put the wrapped bone in the pot 15 minutes before the end of cooking.

6 When the meat is cooked, take it out of the pot, remove the string, slice and place on a heated serving dish. Drain the vegetables, discarding the bouquet garni, and arrange around the meat; keep hot.

7 Slice the bread and toast on both sides. Meanwhile, lift out and unwrap the marrowbone, scoop out the marrow, then spread on the hot toast.

8 Serve the broth separately with the toast, followed by the platter of meat and vegetables. Traditional accompaniments include dill pickles, pickled onions, mustard and horseradish sauce.

Serves 6–8

17

Four-meat Hotpot Soup

3 lbs. stewing beef
1 lb. salt pork
1 Cornish hen with liver
1 knuckle of veal, with meat on
21 cups water
coarse salt
pepper
1½ lbs. carrots
4 onions
3 cloves garlic
4 cloves
1½ lbs. leeks
1 celeriac root
1-2 bulbs of fennel
1 bouquet garni

For the forcemeat roll:
½ lb. salt pork
1 shallot
3 cloves garlic
4 cups fresh white breadcrumbs
¼ cup brown stock
1 egg

1 Wipe the various meats and derind the salt pork. Tie the beef with string. Split the hen in half and wash the liver. Put the water in a large pot, add a good handful of coarse salt and some pepper; put in the beef, bring to a boil, with the lid off, remove the scum from the surface, cover, reduce the heat and simmer for 1 hour.

2 Meanwhile, peel the carrots, onions and garlic; stud the onions with the cloves. Trim and wash the leeks, celeriac root and fennel; cut them in quarters.

3 When the beef has cooked for 1 hour, add the knuckle of veal, the hen and salt pork. Bring to a boil again, skim the surface, cover and reduce the heat and cook for 1 hour longer.

4 Meanwhile, prepare the forcemeat roll. Cut the salt pork into tiny pieces; peel and finely chop the shallot and remaining garlic. Chop the liver. Put all the forcemeat ingredients in a mixing bowl, moisten with the stock and mix together well. Season well with salt and pepper.

5 Sprinkle a piece of cheesecloth with a little flour. Place the forcemeat in the center, fold over the cloth and mold into a sausage shape. Tie the ends with string.

6 After 2 hours of cooking, put the forcemeat roll into the pot together with the prepared vegetables, garlic and bouquet garni and simmer for 1 hour longer.

7 Wrap the marrowbones in cheesecloth and tie securely; put in the pot about 15 minutes before the end of cooking.

8 Serve the Four-meat Hotpot as for Hotpot Soup (see previous page), with the broth served separately, the meats carved into portions on one platter, with the toasted slices of bread, and the vegetables on another with slices of forcemeat around them.

Serves 6–8

Four-meat Hotpot Soup — a satisfying dish for family appetites

Cockie-Leekie

3 leeks
1 branch celery
1 carrot
2 lbs. chicken
6¼ cups chicken stock
2 tablespoons butter
salt and pepper
2 tablespoons finely chopped
  parsley

1 Trim the outer leaves of the leeks to within 2 inches of the white stems and cut away the roots. Split the leeks in half lengthwise, wash them well, then cut into chunks. Wash and cut the celery into ½-inch lengths; peel and slice the carrot.

2 Wipe the chicken and wash its giblets well. Put both into a large deep pan, add the stock and simmer for 1 hour or until the chicken is tender. Discard the giblets; take out the chicken, remove the skin and take the meat off the bones. Leave the broth to cool, then chill and remove the fat from the surface.

3 Heat the butter in a large pan, put in the leeks, celery and carrot; add salt and pepper to taste. Cover the pan and cook gently until the leeks are soft but not colored (about 10 minutes). Add the chicken broth and the pieces of chicken meat, increase the heat, cover the pan and simmer for about 15 minutes. Serve at once, garnished with chopped parsley.

Tip: This soup is improved by making the day before and chilling overnight; then remove the fat the next day and complete the recipe.

Serves 6–8

For this traditional Scottish soup, a chicken (cockie) is poached in stock, the meat taken off the bones, returned to the broth with leeks (leekie); celery and carrot may also be added to vary the flavor

Soup Garnishes

Bacon
Crumble crisply-fried slices and sprinkle over soup.

Pasta
Either cook in the soup toward the end of cooking or cook separately and add to the hot soup.

Croûtes
Remove crusts from slices of French bread, spread with butter (flavored if liked) or grated cheese on one side. Bake until crisp and golden.

Croûtons
Remove crusts from slices of bread, cut into $\frac{1}{4}$–$\frac{1}{2}$-inch cubes and either fry in hot butter or oil until golden and crisp, or toast them.

Melba Toast
Remove crusts from $\frac{1}{4}$-inch thick slices of white bread. Toast until a pale brown, then cut through the middle of each to give extra-thin slices. Toast again, white sides up, until golden. Or bake the thinly-cut slices in the bottom of a very slow oven until very crisp and curled; then brown under broiler.

Sippets
Remove crusts from slices of bread, cut into large triangles and bake in a slow oven till dry and very crisp.

Dumplings or Meatballs
Add either plain or flavored ones to the soup toward the end of cooking and simmer for about 20 minutes.

Herbs and Green Stems
Sprinkle over soups finely chopped herbs, green celery leaves, chives or the green stems of scallions, all either snipped with scissors or chopped.

Mushrooms
Thinly slice and gently sauté in butter for 5 minutes until soft but not colored. Sprinkle on just before serving.

Borsch

2 carrots
2 leeks
4 onions
2 cloves
2 cups diced beets
1 white cabbage
2 lbs. beef bottom round
1 marrowbone
1 bouquet garni
1 fennel branch or pinch of ground cumin
$\frac{1}{4}$ cup tomato paste
salt and pepper
1 lb. cooked garlic sausage
5 pickles (dill)
$1\frac{1}{4}$ cups sour cream

1 Scrape the carrots and cut into small rounds. Clean and chop the leeks. Peel the onions, stud 1 whole onion with cloves and cut the other onions into very fine slices. Peel the beets and chop finely. Cut away the core and stalks, then shred the cabbage.

2 Fill a large saucepan two-thirds with water. Boil. Add the meat and the marrowbone, return to a boil and skim off the scum from the surface as it rises. Add the leeks, the carrots, the onions, the bouquet garni, beets, cabbage and fennel or cumin.

3 Thin the tomato paste with a few tablespoons of hot soup. Pour this back into the pan, season with salt and pepper and bring to a boil. Cover, reduce the heat and simmer for $2\frac{1}{2}$ hours. Remove the meat and marrowbone from the pot, then chop the beef finely.

4 Slice the garlic sausage and the pickles. Add the meat, the garlic sausage and the pickles to the soup. Cover and simmer for about 30 minutes. Heat a soup tureen.

5 Lift the bouquet garni and the clove-studded onion out of the soup. Pour the soup into the warmed tureen. Serve the cream in a sauce boat, allowing a generous spoonful per serving.

Serves 4–6

Pirojkis (Pirogis)

For the pastry:
$2\frac{3}{4}$ cups flour
$\frac{2}{3}$ cup butter
2 eggs plus 1 egg yolk, beaten
pinch salt

For the filling:
3 eggs
8 ozs. cream cheese
2 sprigs parsley
salt and pepper
nutmeg
$\frac{1}{2}$ cup butter

1 To make the pastry: put the flour onto a board or into a bowl and make a well in the center. Cut up the butter. Break the eggs and put with the salt and butter into the well. Mix all together to form a firm and elastic dough. Roll this out with a rolling pin several times, folding between rollings.

2 Prepare the filling. Put 2 of the eggs set aside for the filling into a saucepan of cold water. Bring to a boil. Simmer gently for 10 minutes over moderate heat so the shells do not break. Remove from the boiling water and cool in cold water: they will then be easier to shell.

3 Put the cream cheese into a bowl. Wash and chop the parsley. Add, with the salt, pepper and a little grated nutmeg, to the cream cheese.

4 Put the hard-boiled eggs through a grinder and add to the cream cheese. Blend well together to form a smooth, even mixture. Put the butter in a bowl and cream well before blending with cream cheese-egg mixture.

5 Dust the board or the table work surface with flour. Roll out the pastry to a thickness of about $\frac{1}{8}$

inch. Then cut out circles of 2½-3 inches in diameter.

6 On one side of each circle put 2 tablespoons of the filling and cover with the other half to form a turnover. Dampen the edges and press together to seal. Preheat the oven to 400°F.

7 Brush the turnovers with the yolk to glaze them. Bake in the oven for 20 minutes. Serve hot as an accompaniment to Borsch.

All varieties of borsch (below), also spelled bortsch and borscht, contain root vegetables: the name comes from the old slavic word for beet. The classic accompaniment are pirojkis (also pirogis and pirozhki—from the old word for feast) often filled with meat from the soup

Onion Soup with Blue Cheese

1 lb. onions
2 shallots
2 cloves garlic
½ cup butter
2 tablespoons olive oil
6¼ cups brown stock
6 rounds French bread
⅛ lb. blue cheese
2 tablespoons brandy
¾ cup grated Romano cheese
1 cup finely chopped walnuts
salt and pepper

1 Peel and chop the onions and the shallots; peel and crush the garlic.

2 Heat one-third of the butter and the oil in a sauté pan. Add the chopped onions and shallots and let them brown while stirring with a wooden spoon.

3 When the onions and the shallots are golden, add the stock. Bring to a boil and simmer for 40 minutes.

4 Twenty minutes before it is ready, heat the oven to 400°F. Put the bread in it to dry. Mash the blue cheese and most of the rest of the butter in a bowl with a fork, reserving a little butter for the bread. Moisten this mixture with the brandy. Heat the broiler.

5 Butter the bread. Spread on the grated cheese.

6 Add the softened blue cheese and the crushed walnuts to the soup. Let it boil for about 3 minutes.

7 Rub the crushed garlic over the inside surface of an earthenware bowl. Pour the soup into it. Adjust the seasoning and be very generous with the pepper.

8 Put the slices of bread on top of the soup and brown quickly under the broiler. Serve piping hot.

Serves 6

Cheesy Mushroom Soup

12 ozs. mushrooms
juice ½ lemon
¼ cup butter
salt and pepper
few slices stale bread
4¼ cups chicken stock
½ cup port
1 lean slice cooked ham
1 cup grated Romano cheese

1 Cut off the ends of the mushrooms stalks. Wash the mushrooms carefully without soaking them, then slice them finely. Sprinkle the mushrooms with the lemon juice.

2 Melt the butter in a saucepan and when it is hot, sauté the mushrooms for 10 minutes. Season with salt and pepper.

3 Heat the broiler and toast the bread on both sides.

4 Add the chicken stock and the port to the mushrooms. Bring to a boil and cook for 5 minutes. Chop the ham and add it at the end of the 5 minutes.

5 Pour the very hot soup into individual flameproof bowls. Arrange the slices of toast on the surface of the soup and sprinkle generously with the grated cheese. Broil until the cheese browns. Serve the soup at once.

Serves 4

Crushed walnuts and blue cheese add a delicious zest to onion soup. Top with cheesy croûtes to serve

Corn Chowder

¼ lb. salt pork
1 onion
2 medium potatoes
2 branches celery
1 red pepper
2 tablespoons butter
2¼ cups white stock or water
1 bay leaf
salt and pepper to taste
2 tablespoons flour
2¼ cups milk
2 cups corn
1 tablespoon finely chopped
   parsley

1 Dice the salt pork, put in a pan with cold water to cover and blanch by bringing to a boil and boiling for about 1 minute; then drain and set aside. Peel and chop the onion; peel and dice the potatoes; chop the celery; cut the pepper in half, remove the seeds and membrane and chop.

2 Heat the butter in a large pan, then put in the diced salt pork and fry till it starts to brown. Add the celery and onion and cook for 1 minute. Add the diced potatoes and red pepper, the white stock or water, the bay leaf and salt and pepper, bring to a boil, cover, reduce the heat and simmer for 15 minutes or until the potatoes are almost tender.

3 Blend the flour to a paste with a little of the cold milk. Stir this into the hot soup. Add the remaining milk and the corn, bring to a boil to thicken, then cover, reduce the heat and simmer for about 10 minutes or until the corn is tender. Remove the bay leaf. Check for seasoning, sprinkle with parsley and serve.

Serves 6

Chowders are thick fish, meat or vegetable soups cum stews; the most famous is New England Clam Chowder shown at right

New England Clam Chowder

1 lb. fresh steamer clams or
   canned minced clams
3 small potatoes
3 slices bacon
1 medium onion
2¾ cups milk
1 cup heavy cream
1 tablespoon butter
salt if necessary
freshly ground black pepper

1 Scrub the fresh clams and soak in three changes of cold water to remove any sand. Steam them over 1 cup water for 8 minutes until they open. Discard the shells and chop the clams into small pieces. Strain the broth through cheesecloth to remove the sand.

2 Peel and dice the potatoes; derind and cut the bacon into small pieces. Peel and finely chop the onion. Boil the potatoes in salted water for 15 minutes.

3 Fry the bacon in a saucepan until 1 tablespoon of fat has been rendered. Remove the bacon pieces and set aside, then sauté the onion in the fat for 5 minutes. Add the strained clam broth or the liquid from the canned clams. Simmer for 5 minutes. Add the chopped clams, milk, cream, butter and potatoes. Season with salt and simmer for 5 minutes or until the potatoes are tender.

4 Ladle the chowder into individual bowls and garnish each with a sprinkling of black pepper and the bacon pieces.

Serves 6

Sausage and Cabbage Soup

1 lb. cabbage
1 clove garlic
2 tablespoons butter
3 tablespoons flour
5 cups chicken stock
salt and pepper
6-8 frankfurters

1 Cut away the core from the cabbage; shred finely. Peel and crush the garlic. Heat the fat in a pan and soften the cabbage and garlic in it — about 10 minutes.

2 Mix in the flour, then gradually blend in the stock, stirring all the time. Bring to a boil, season with salt and pepper, reduce the heat, cover and simmer 1 hour.

3 Meanwhile, slice the frankfurters thinly. When the soup is ready, skim any fat off the surface, add the sliced frankfurters, leave 5 minutes to heat through and serve.

Serves 4-6

Lentil Soup

1 lb. lentils
1 onion
1 carrot
8 strips bacon
¼ lb. butter
1 bouquet garni
4¼ cups chicken stock
salt and pepper

1 Wash the lentils and put them in a pan. Cover them with cold water and bring to a boil. Boil for 1 minute, then drain the lentils. Wash the pan.

2 Peel and chop the onion and the carrot. Dice the bacon.

3 Melt half the butter in the rinsed-out pan and add the bacon, onion and carrot. Sauté for 10 minutes, then add the lentils, bouquet garni, salt and pepper. Pour in the stock, bring to a boil, then reduce the heat, cover and simmer for about 50 minutes or until the lentils are soft.

4 When the soup is cooked, take out the bouquet garni and purée the soup in a blender or work through a strainer or food mill. When smooth, pour into a pan and then reheat.

5 Just before serving, heat up a soup tureen. Pour the hot soup into it. Cut the rest of the butter into small pieces. Add them to the soup and mix in well. Serve very hot, with bread croûtons, lightly rubbed with garlic and fried in butter.

Serves 4

Tomato and Onion Soup

3 medium onions
1 large clove garlic
2 ripe medium tomatoes
1 small celery heart
5 cups bouillon
3 tablespoons olive oil
salt and freshly ground pepper
few sprigs chervil
½ cup grated Cheddar

1 Peel the onions and garlic. Slice the onions finely. Chop the garlic. Skin the tomatoes, then quarter and remove the seeds. Trim and chop the celery heart.

2 Bring the stock to a boil. Heat the oil in a pan. Add the onion rings and fry until golden. Add the tomatoes and garlic and cook until soft, stirring with a wooden spoon. Add the celery, and the hot stock. Season to taste.

3 Cook the onion soup slowly with the lid on for about 30 minutes.

4 Rinse, drain and finely chop the chervil. Preheat the oven to 450°F.

5 When the soup is cooked, add the chopped chervil. Pour it into a casserole, preferably an earthenware one. Sprinkle with grated cheese and brown in the oven for about 10 minutes. Serve immediately.

Serves 4

Scotch Broth

2 lbs. stewing lamb, with bones
6 cups cold water
3 tablespoons barley
2 onions
2 carrots
2 branches celery
1 bay leaf
½ teaspoon thyme
3 tablespoons finely chopped
   parsley
½ teaspoon salt
freshly ground black pepper

1 Peel and chop the onions; peel and dice the carrots; trim and dice the celery. Trim and wipe the lamb.

2 Put the lamb into a pan with the water. Bring to a boil, reduce the heat, cover and simmer for 1 hour. Then add the remaining ingredients and simmer for a further 1 hour. Add more water if necessary.

3 Discard the bay leaf. Lift out the lamb with a slotted spoon and separate the meat from the bone. Discard the bones and cut the meat into small pieces. Add the meat to the soup. Simmer for 5 minutes. Serve hot.

Serves 6

Lentils are rich in protein and form the basis of a cheap and filling soup (right). Garnish with garlic-flavored sippets — triangles of bread baked in the oven

Clear Soups

Consommé is probably the best known clear soup. Prime quality beef, herbs and vegetables are simmered in a well-flavored brown stock, and the addition of egg whites — sometimes crushed eggshells are used as well — help to clarify the liquid. The mixture is then strained, with the crust that has formed on top during the cooking acting as a filter.

To be sure of making a sparkling clear soup, which all consommés must be, all utensils and ingredients — especially the stock — must be completely free from grease.

You can serve consommé hot or cold (in which case it is lightly jellied and usually chopped), and plain or varied by adding different garnishes. A consommé, in fact, takes its name from the garnish, and this should always be cooked or prepared separately and added only at the moment of serving. That way nothing can cloud and spoil the appearance of the soup.

Beef Consommé

1 carrot
1 leek, green part only
2 branches celery
4 ripe tomatoes (optional)
2 egg whites
1 lb. prime lean ground beef
few sprigs chervil and tarragon
8½ cups chilled brown stock
¾ cup cold water
peppercorns
1 tablespoon sherry (optional)

1 Remove all fat from the surface of the brown stock and turn into a large pan. Peel the carrot. Wash and dry it, together with the leek, celery and tomatoes, if used. Chop or slice them. Wash, dry and chop the herbs.

2 Mix the vegetables with the egg whites in a large bowl; stir in the beef, tomatoes, chopped herbs and the water.

3 Add the vegetable mixture to the stock, mix together, then bring slowly to a boil, stirring to the bottom of the pan to prevent the mixture from sticking. Keep whisking the mixture until a thick froth starts to form.

4 As soon as the mixture starts to boil, turn down the heat and simmer, covered, for about 1½ hours without stirring. From time to time remove any fat which rises to the surface (there should be hardly any at all).

5 At the end of the cooking time, pour the contents of the pan through a scalded cloth over a strainer, on which the peppercorns have been put, into a bowl underneath. At first hold back the egg white crust with a spoon, then let it slip onto the cloth. Pour the soup through again and over the egg white filter. The consommé should now be completely clear. Reheat, check the seasoning and add the sherry, if liked, to improve the flavor.

Serves 8

Variations:

Consommé Colbert: add ½ cup port to the above quantity of hot soup; add cooked diced carrots and turnips, cooked garden peas, as well as a poached egg per serving.

Consommé Julienne: add cooked matchstick-thin strips of vegetables (carrot, turnip, celery) to the hot soup.

Consommé à la Brunoise: add a mixture of cooked small diced carrots, green beans or celery to the hot soup. Substitute chicken stock for the brown stock if liked.

Consommé à la Madrilène: substitute chicken stock for brown stock; blanch a few tarragon leaves in boiling water for 2 minutes, then add to the hot soup. Float a thin slice of lemon in each bowl.

Consommé au Riz: add a small quantity of cooked long grain rice to the hot soup.

Consommé au Vermicelli: add vermicelli or other tiny pasta to the soup while reheating.

Quick Consommé

Heat canned consommé gently in a pan and stir in 1 tablespoon sherry or Madeira or to taste to boost the flavor. Garnish and serve as for homemade consommé.

Watercress Soup

½ bunch watercress
⅛ lb. lean pork
1-2 scallions
2¾ cups chicken stock
½ teaspoon grated fresh gingerroot
½ teaspoon soy sauce
1 teaspoon dry sherry
salt and pepper

1 Wash and dry the watercress. Reserve 4 small top clusters for garnish. Remove the thick stems and cut the rest up roughly. Cut the pork into very small slivers; trim and thinly slice the scallions.

2 Put into a pan the chicken stock, gingerroot, soy sauce, sherry, the pork, sliced scallions and salt and pepper to taste. Remember the stock is already well seasoned.

3 Bring to a boil, cover and simmer for 15 minutes. Add the watercress and simmer the soup for 3 more minutes. Serve at once, garnishing each bowl with a sprig of watercress.

Serves 4

Look 'n Cook Clarification of Consommé

1 Ingredients: chilled brown stock, carrots, celery, green part of 1 leek, tomatoes, chervil and tarragon, eggs, ground beef **2** Carefully remove any fat from the surface of the stock **3** Chop or slice the vegetables and tomatoes; wash and chop the herbs **4** Put the prepared vegetables and herbs into a large bowl together with the ground beef. Add the egg whites only **5** Mix the ingredients together well, adding a little cold water to moisten. Add the vegetable mixture to the stock and heat gently, stirring all the time **6** As soon as it begins to boil, reduce the heat so it is only just simmering. Skim off any fat that rises to the surface — there should be hardly any at all — and cook for 1½ hours without stirring; this will allow a 'crust' to form on top **7** Scald a cloth and place over a large strainer; put the peppercorns on the cloth, then slowly pour the soup over the vegetable/egg white mixture to clarify **8** and **9** Two garnishes for consommé: vermicelli and chopped tomatoes.

Cold Soups

Cold Spanish Soup (Gazpacho)

1 cucumber
salt
1½ cups dry white breadcrumbs
3 tomatoes
1 clove garlic
4 tablespoons olive oil
1 tablespoon lemon juice
2¼ cups cold water
salt and pepper
pinch cayenne pepper
2 mild Spanish onions
1 green pepper
bunch chervil
bunch chives

1 Peel the cucumber with a potato peeler. Dice it. Bring a saucepan of salted water to a boil. Add half the diced cucumber and leave to simmer for 10 minutes. Sprinkle salt over the rest of the cucumber to draw out some of its moisture.

2 Drain the cooked cucumber. Purée in a blender or food mill or rub through a strainer. Put the breadcrumbs into a bowl. Add just enough water to moisten them. Skin the tomatoes, then cut half the tomatoes into small pieces.

3 Peel and chop the garlic and put into a mortar. Add a pinch of salt and pound with the pestle. Add the tomato pieces and breadcrumbs. Pound until the mixture is thoroughly blended. Add the oil a little at a time, mixing all the time. Add the lemon juice and cucumber purée. Dilute with the cold water, stirring all the time. Add salt and pepper to taste and a pinch of cayenne pepper. Mix again, then chill in the refrigerator for at least 2 hours.

4 Chop the rest of the tomatoes into small cubes. Peel the onions and chop roughly. Wash the green pepper. Dry it and cut in half. Remove the seeds and white membrane, then cut the flesh into small cubes. Rinse the cucumber cubes. Squeeze them gently with your hands to make sure they are well drained. Wash and dry the chervil and the chives. Chop them.

5 Arrange the tomatoes, onions, green pepper and cucumber in 4 separate dishes. Divide the soup into 4 individual bowls. Sprinkle the chervil and chives over them. Serve very chilled.

Serves 4

Tip: Each guest puts a little of all the finely chopped raw vegetables into his soup bowl. It is customary to put an ice cube into each soup bowl at the moment of serving.

Gazpacho or gaspacho (below), is a Spanish salad-soup made with a purée of cucumber, tomatoes, garlic, breadcrumbs, and oil. Served chilled, the soup is garnished with herbs and accompanied by bowls of chopped tomato, green peppers, onion and cucumber.

Vichyssoise

3½ cups chicken stock
½ teaspoon salt
4 medium potatoes
3 medium onions
3 leeks (or 1 extra onion)
½ teaspoon fresh chervil or marjoram
2 tablespoons fresh parsley
½ cup heavy cream

1 Put the chicken stock in a large pan and bring to simmering point; add the salt. Peel the potatoes and cut into medium chunks. Peel and chop the onions. Prepare, wash, dry and slice the leeks. Add all these vegetables to the stock, bring to a boil, cover, reduce the heat and simmer for about 20 minutes.

2 Cool a little, then put the soup in a blender and blend until smooth or pass through a food mill or strainer. Chill for at least 2 hours.

3 Wash, dry and finely chop the chervil or marjoram and the parsley. Just before serving add the herbs and cream. If wished, put 2 or 3 overlapping raw onion rings in the center of each soup dish when serving.

Serves 6

To Store Soup
Unthickened soup (no thickener has been added) freezes best and can be frozen in handy quantities for up to 3 months. Cool, then skim off any fat from the surface before freezing a soup; allow about ½ inch headspace for expansion.

Vichyssoise (below) is one of the classic French soups. Traditionally garnished with snipped chives, try finely chopped parsley or a few raw onion rings instead

Avocado Soup

2 large plus 1 small avocados
½ teaspoon salt
pinch white pepper
1 cup heavy cream
3½ cups chicken stock
3 tablespoons dry sherry

1 Peel the 2 large avocados, remove the pits and cut the flesh into small pieces. Put it into a blender with salt, pepper and half the cream and blend until smooth or work through a strainer. Then add the remaining cream and blend again until mixed.

2 Heat the chicken stock until it is warm but not hot. Pour in the avocado cream mixture. Taste and adjust the seasoning. Chill this in the refrigerator for 1 hour.

3 Stir in the sherry. Peel the small avocado, remove the pit and cut the flesh into thin slices. Add to the soup and serve.

Serves 4–6

Tip: Do not make this soup too early in the day. Avocado discolors when exposed to the air so put into a covered container when chilling. A little lemon juice brushed over the flesh helps to prevent discoloration.

Watercress and Potato Soup

1 bunch watercress
2 tablespoons butter
1 onion
1 branch celery
2 medium potatoes
2¾ cups chicken stock
1 tablespoon lemon juice
½ teaspoon salt
freshly ground black pepper
½ cup heavy cream

1 Wash the watercress and reserve some of the leaves for decoration. Chop the remainder and the stems into small pieces.

2 Melt the butter in a saucepan. Peel the onion and chop it finely. Clean the celery and chop it. Peel the potatoes and cut into cubes. Add the onion and celery to the pan and cook for 3 minutes.

3 Add the potatoes, stock, chopped watercress, lemon juice, salt and pepper. Cover and simmer for 30 minutes. Remove from the heat and cool a little.

4 Work through a strainer or purée in a blender. Then strain the soup into a container with a lid. Taste and adjust seasoning if necessary. Cover and chill for 2 hours. Just before serving stir in the cream and the reserved watercress.

Serves 4

Cream of Lettuce Soup

3 heads lettuce
2 tablespoons butter
1½ teaspoons salt

freshly ground black pepper
3½ cups water
½ cup heavy cream
juice ½ lemon
6 scallions

1 Cut the lettuce into quarters, remove the cores and wash the leaves. Cook in boiling, salted water for 10 minutes. Drain and then chop roughly.

2 Melt the butter in a saucepan, add the chopped lettuce, put on the lid, then tip it a little and cook slowly for 5 minutes. Season the lettuce with salt and pepper, add the water and bring to a boil. Cover, lower the heat and simmer for 1 hour. Cool a little.

3 Pour the soup into a blender and blend until smooth, or rub through a strainer. Taste and adjust the seasoning.

4 Chill the soup very well and, just before serving, stir in first the cream and then the lemon juice.

5 Trim the scallions, leaving about 1 inch of the green part still on them. With a pair of kitchen scissors or a sharp knife, cut this

---

Avocados, combined with sherry and cream, make an excellent soup

green part downward, into as many thin strips as possible. Put 1 onion in the center of each bowl of soup so that the thin strips float.

6 Serve very cold.

Serves 6

Chilled Cucumber and Tomato Soup

6⅓ cups chicken stock
⅓ cup long grain rice
4 very ripe tomatoes
½ cucumber
½ cup heavy cream
small bunch chervil
pinch cayenne pepper
salt and pepper

1 Bring the stock to a boil in a saucepan. Wash the rice and add to the vigorously boiling stock; cook 20 minutes.

2 Wash and skin the tomatoes; quarter and squeeze gently to extract the water and seeds. Add tomatoes to the stock after the rice has cooked for 20 minutes. Let cook 30 minutes longer.

3 Remove the end of the cucumber. Cut in two, lengthwise; take out seeds with a small spoon. Cut in thin strips.

4 When cooked, purée the soup in a blender or rub through a strainer. Stiffly whip and fold in cream. Add cayenne pepper. Mix well together. Taste and adjust the seasoning; cool.

5 When cold, add the cucumber strips. Stir. Chill in refrigerator for at least 3 hours. About 5 minutes before serving, wash, dry and chop the chervil. Ladle the chilled soup into individual bowls. Sprinkle on the chervil and serve.

Serves 4

Chilled Cucumber and Tomato Soup, garnished with strips of cucumber

Borsch, Chilled

2 cups diced beets (7-8 medium-
 size beets)
2½ cups beet liquid
1 cup beef stock
1 tablespoon grated onion
1 tablespoon lemon juice
½ teaspoon salt

For the garnish:
sliced hard-boiled eggs (½ egg per
 person)
peeled, sliced cucumber
sour cream

1 Scrub beets and cut stems no
shorter than 1 inch from the top so
that the beets won't bleed.

2 In water to cover boil beets until
tender (approximately 45 minutes).
Eggs may be boiled in the same pan
and removed after 20 minutes.

3 Save the beet water. Drain beets
and place them in cold water. Slip
off skins.

4 Add 2½ cups beet water to the
beef stock.

5 Blend 1 cup beets with 1 cup
beef-beet liquid. Repeat with other
cup of beets.

6 Stir blended beets and remaining
liquid together. Add onion, lemon
juice and salt.

7 Chill at least 2 hours. Stir and
garnish before serving.

Serves 4

Minted Pea Soup, Chilled

2 cups chicken stock
1 cup water
¼ cup mint (3 large sprigs)
3 cups peas (fresh)
¼ cup diced onion
½ cup heavy cream
salt to taste

For the garnish:
whipped cream and fresh mint
 leaves

1 Bring chicken stock, water and
mint to a boil.

2 Drop peas and onions into rapidly boiling stock.

3 Cover and cook peas at a slow
boil until tender (no longer than 12
minutes).

4 Cool and work through a food
mill, using the finest disc. (Note: a
blender will not do in this case. The
outer skins of some peas are tough
and won't blend well.)

5 Stir the cream into the purée.

6 Salt to taste.

7 Chill the soup in a pitcher.

8 If the soup separates, simply stir
it well before pouring into chilled
bowls.

9 Top with whipped cream and a
small mint leaf sprig.

Serves 4

Fruit Soup, Chilled

½ cup raisins
½ cup prunes, cooked, pitted and
 chopped
½ cup dried apricots, chopped
1 cup dry red wine
2 cups cold water
1-lb. can tart pitted cherries with
 juice
2 tart cooking apples, peeled and
 diced
1 cinnamon stick
⅓ cup sugar
½ teaspoon grated orange or lemon
 rind
2 tablespoons cornstarch
½ cup cold water
sugar to taste

For the garnish:
½ cup heavy cream, whipped with 1
 teaspoon confectioners' sugar

1 Soak dried fruit in red wine and
water for 1 hour.

2 Place all fruit in large heavy
saucepan with the liquid.

3 Add cinnamon stick and sugar
and boil 15 minutes (or until apples
are soft but not mushy).

4 Mix cornstarch with ½ cup cold
water and add this mixture to soup.

5 If soup is too tart, add more
sugar. Add grated orange or lemon
rind.

6 Cook soup 2 minutes at slow
boil.

7 Chill soup thoroughly. (May be
put in freezer until chilled only.)

8 Serve in chilled glass bowls or
compôtes with dollops of whipped
cream and a sprinkle of nutmeg,
cinnamon, and grated orange or
lemon rind.

Serves 6–8

Granville Soup
(with Blueberries)

2 cups white wine
2 slices lemon
2 cups water
½ cup sugar
¼ teaspoon salt
⅓ cup tapioca
2 cinnamon sticks
½ cup raspberry and ½ cup currant
 jelly
1 cup grape juice
2 cups fresh blueberries

1 Combine all except blueberries
and leave to stand about 5 minutes.

2 Bring to a boil and stir often.

3 Cover and very gently simmer
about 15-20 minutes, then remove
from heat. Stir in blueberries and
chill well.

4 Remove lemon slice and cinnamon stick.

5 Serve in soup dishes with un-
salted unwhipped heavy cream
floating on top.

Serves 6

Creamy Soups

All creamy soups have a smooth, velvety texture achieved by thickening them with cream or egg yolks, flour or some kind of cereal. They can be made with stock or milk or combinations of both.

Green vegetables are popular choices for cream soups; they are usually cooked in milk, then strained and blended and then thickened.

If both egg yolks and cream are used for thickening a soup, the extra velvety consistency achieved is called a *velouté*.

Bisque is a term applied to shellfish soups only. Often a bisque is enriched by the addition of a special butter made with the lobster roe, and in some cases the shells themselves are pounded and incorporated as well to give an extra fishy flavor.

To Thicken Soups

If using cream: put in a bowl, blend in a little of the hot but not boiling soup, then stir back into the pan of soup and reheat but do not boil.

If using egg yolk: blend with a little cold milk or cream in a bowl, mix in a little of the hot soup, then strain back into the pan of soup; reheat very gently but do not boil or else the egg will curdle (if the soup already contains flour/cereal, curdling is less likely to occur).

If using flour or fine cereal: blend with a little cold milk or other liquid in a bowl, mix in a little hot soup, then pour back into the pan, bring to a boil and cook for a few minutes until thickened.

Cream of Spinach Soup

2 lbs. leaf spinach
1 small onion
2 tablespoons butter
4 tablespoons flour
1¼ cups white stock
1¼ cups milk
salt and pepper

1 Wash the spinach well; peel and finely chop the onion. Put the spinach in a large pan with about 2 tablespoons water and cook until tender — about 5 minutes. Drain well and rub through a strainer or work through a food mill; set aside.

2 Heat the butter in a saucepan; put in the onion and cook until soft and transparent. Stir in the flour and blend. Pour in the white stock and milk, a little at a time, stirring continuously until smooth.

3 Stir in the spinach purée, season to taste, cook gently for a few minutes until hot, then serve immediately.

Serves 4–6

Cream of Spinach Soup is a delicious way of serving this underrated vegetable

Cream of Chervil Soup

  ★ ⧗

3 tablespoons butter
5 tablespoons flour
6⅓ cups chicken or white stock
salt and pepper
1 egg yolk
¼ cup heavy cream
2 tablespoons finely chopped
    chervil or parsley

1 Melt the butter in a large saucepan. Blend in the flour to make a roux. Pour in the stock a little at a time, and stir continuously over medium heat until the sauce is thick and smooth. Season with salt and pepper to taste.

2 Mix the egg yolk with the cream in a bowl; stir in a little of the hot liquid, then pour into the pan of soup, stirring continuously. Add the chervil, or parsley, reheat gently but do not boil, and serve at once.

Serves 4–6

Cream of Leek and Potato Soup

  ★ ⧗

3 leeks, white part only
2 large potatoes
2 tablespoons butter
8½ cups white stock
salt and pepper
1 egg yolk
½ cup heavy cream
2 handfuls chervil or parsley

1 Wash the leeks well (this is best done by standing them, green stems down, in a jug of cold water so grit and dirt can float out from between the stems). Drain them and cut into thin slices. Peel the potatoes and cut into quarters.

2 In a pan, melt the butter. When hot add the leek slices. Soften them a little in the covered pan, stirring frequently over gentle heat.

3 Take the pan off the heat and pour in the stock. Return to the heat and bring to a boil again. Add salt and pepper. Put in the potato quarters, cover the pan, reduce the heat and simmer about 20 minutes till tender. Then purée in a blender or work through a strainer or food mill.

4 In a bowl blend the cream and egg yolk together, then stir in some of the hot soup. Return this mixture to the soup. Stir and adjust the seasoning, adding plenty of pepper. Heat gently for a few moments but do not boil.

5 Meanwhile, wash and dry the chervil or parsley, then chop it finely.

6 Pour the soup into a heated tureen. Sprinkle with the chopped herbs and serve.

Serves 6

Cream of Chicken Soup

  ★

3 tablespoons butter
5 tablespoons flour
3⅔ cups chicken stock
½ cup finely chopped cooked
    chicken
¼ teaspoon salt
freshly ground black pepper

For the thickening:
1 egg yolk
¼ cup heavy cream

1 Melt the butter in a large pan. Stir in the flour to make a roux and cook for about 1 minute without coloring. Then take the pan off the heat and gradually blend in the chicken stock, stirring all the time to make a smooth sauce. Return the pan to the heat and bring to a boil.

2 Reduce the heat, then add the cooked chicken, salt and pepper and cook for 2 minutes.

3 Blend the egg yolk and cream together in a bowl. Stir in a little of the hot soup, then return to the pan and reheat gently, stirring all the time, until thickened. Do not allow the soup to boil after the egg yolk is added. Serve at once.

Serves 4

Cream of Mushroom Soup

  ★

1 lb. mushrooms
1 shallot
4 tablespoons butter
2 tablespoons flour
6⅓ cups brown stock
salt and pepper
1 egg yolk
2 tablespoons heavy cream
juice ½ lemon

1 Wipe the mushrooms and slice them finely. Peel and chop the shallot.

2 Heat the butter in a large pan; when hot add the shallot and sauté quickly till golden. Then add the sliced mushrooms and sauté over medium heat for about 4 minutes. Stir in the flour and cook for a further 2 minutes, then blend in the brown stock off the heat. Return the pan to the heat, season with salt and pepper to taste and cook gently for about 10 minutes.

3 To thicken the soup, blend the egg yolk with the cream and the lemon juice, then stir into the hot soup. Reheat very gently but do not boil. Serve at once.

Serves 4–6

Cream of Mushroom Soup — as a variation try stirring in plain yogurt instead of cream

34

Avgolemono (Greek Egg and Lemon Soup)

7½ cups chicken stock
½ cup long grain rice, vermicelli or other pasta
3 eggs
juice 2 small lemons
salt and freshly ground black pepper

1 Bring the chicken stock to a boil. Add the rice, vermicelli or pasta and simmer for 15 minutes.

2 Meanwhile, beat the eggs until frothy. Slowly add the lemon juice to the eggs, beating constantly. Add about a quarter of the hot stock, 1 tablespoon at a time, beating all the time. Remove the remaining stock from the heat and stir in the egg mixture.

3 Adjust the seasoning as necessary and serve immediately.

Serves 8

Cream of Carrot Soup

2 medium onions
2 medium potatoes
2 lbs. carrots
2 tablespoons butter
salt and pepper
8¼ cups white stock
2 tablespoons raw rice

For the thickening:
1 egg yolk
¼ cup heavy cream

1 Peel and slice the onions. Peel and cut the carrots into strips. Peel and dice the potatoes.

2 Melt half the fat in a large pan. When hot, put in the onions and

sauté without coloring over a low heat until soft and translucent.

3 Stir the carrots into the pan. Add the stock and salt to taste, then cover and cook over moderate heat for 30 minutes.

4 Wash the rice under cold running water. Then add the rice and potatoes to the pan and cook for a further 30 minutes. Purée in a blender or work through a strainer or food mill.

5 When the soup is cooked, blend the egg yolk with the cream in a bowl. Season generously with salt and pepper and beat again. Stir in a little of the hot soup; then return the egg yolk mixture to the pan of soup. Reheat gently but do not boil. Serve hot.

Serves 6

Chinese Asparagus Soup

2 onions
2 cups chicken stock
2 tablespoons cornstarch
1 egg
2 tablespoons oil
salt and pepper
1 tablespoon white wine
2 tablespoons cooked tiny peas
3-4 slender, cooked asparagus spears per person

1 Peel and chop up the onions so as to obtain the equivalent of 3 tablespoons. Mix 2 tablespoons of cold water with the cornstarch. Break an egg into a bowl and beat until blended.

2 Heat the oil in the saucepan, put in the chopped onions and sauté slowly until lightly browned. Add the chicken stock with salt and pepper, and mix in the cornstarch, stirring all the time.

3 Then add the wine and peas and bring it to a boil. When the soup starts to thicken, slowly add the

beaten egg, but keep stirring the whole time. When it thickens, remove from the heat.

4 Cut the asparagus into pieces and place them in bowls or soup plates. Add soup and serve.

Serves 4

Cream of Artichoke Soup

3 shallots
6 globe artichokes
juice of 1 lemon
¼ lb. butter
scant ½ cup flour
4¼ cups milk
salt and pepper
½ cup heavy cream

1 Peel and chop the shallots. Remove the artichoke leaves and hairy choke in the center (see page 58). Trim the artichoke hearts and rub them in the lemon juice to stop them turning black. Cut them into quarters.

2 Gently heat 2 tablespoons butter in a pan. Put in the artichoke hearts and the shallots, cover and cook on low heat for 10 minutes.

3 During this time melt the rest of the butter in another pan. Mix in the flour to make a roux and cook for about 2 minutes, but without letting it brown. Remove the pan from the heat and blend in the milk, little by little, beating continuously with a wooden spoon. When smooth return the pan to the heat and bring to a boil; season with salt and pepper and cook gently for 5 minutes.

4 Pour this white sauce over the artichokes and shallot mixture and simmer 30 minutes. Then remove 2 artichoke hearts and dice them. Purée the rest in a blender or work through a strainer or food mill.

5 Heat a soup tureen. Pour in the cream, add the diced artichoke and pour on the hot soup. Stir well and serve immediately.

Serves 4

Cream of Artichoke soup is an unusual way of serving artichokes

Browned Onion Soup with Madeira

3 medium onions
2 cloves garlic
3 tablespoons butter
2 tablespoons oil
¼ cup flour
½ cup dry white wine
salt and pepper
3 egg yolks
¼ cup Madeira
½ French loaf
cayenne pepper
1 cup grated Cheddar cheese

For the bouquet garni:
sprig parsley
good sprig thyme
bay leaf

1 Wash and dry the parsley. Tie the parsley, thyme and bay leaf together, making sure that the thyme and bay leaf are inside the parsley. Peel the onions and chop them. Peel the garlic.

2 Heat the butter and the oil in a sauté pan. Add the chopped onions and cook them, stirring from time to time with a wooden spoon. When they are golden, add the flour and let it cook while stirring until it too turns brown.

3 Pour in the white wine. Let it reduce (evaporate) by half, then add the stock or water. Add salt and plenty of pepper. Add the bouquet garni. Crush the garlic and add it as well. Bring to a boil, then skim. Cover the soup and allow to simmer for about 45 minutes. About 15 minutes before it is ready, preheat the oven to 400°F. to dry out the bread.

4 Mix yolks with the Madeira. Cut the French loaf into thin slices. Spread them on a baking sheet and dry out in the oven. Take out the bread. Heat the broiler.

5 When the soup is cooked, take it off the heat and discard the bouquet garni. When it has stopped bubbling, pour a little of the soup

into the yolk/Madeira mixture, whisking briskly all the time. Then pour it all back into the soup and mix well. Add a hint of cayenne pepper and check the seasoning.

6 Divide the soup among four bowls. Place 2-3 slices of bread in each bowl. Cover the bread with the grated cheese. Stand the bowls in a pan of hot water. Heat on the stove until the water is almost boiling, then brown under the broiler.

7 Serve piping hot as soon as the cheese browns.

Serves 4

Tips: If a soup without onion pieces is preferred, strain it or put through a blender before adding the egg yolks. Don't allow the soup to boil once the egg yolks have been added.

If chopped beet leaves and a potato are added to the onion while frying, the flour would then be unnecessary.

The white wine and Madeira can be replaced with a very full-bodied red wine to produce a 'country' brown soup (gratinée).

Rich Turnip Soup

2 small turnips
4 strips bacon, diced
3 tablespoons butter
¼ lb. sorrel
4¼ cups chicken stock
few sprigs chervil
1 egg yolk
2 tablespoons light cream
salt and pepper

1 Boil 2 small pans of water. Peel and wash the turnips and cut them into cubes. Put the turnips into one pan and the bacon strips into the other. Let each boil for 5 minutes, then drain.

2 Melt the butter in a stewpan. Put the turnips and the bacon into the hot butter and let brown a little on low heat for about 15 minutes.

3 Wash the sorrel and chop it. Add it to the pan and stir in with a wooden spoon, then pour the stock into it and cook for 20 minutes.

4 Wash, dry and chop the chervil. Pour the egg yolk into the soup tureen, add the cream and mix in.

5 When the bacon is cooked, drain. Purée the soup in a blender or work through a strainer or food mill. Taste and adjust the seasoning. Pour the soup into the tureen and beat with a whisk. Add the bacon to the soup and sprinkle it with chervil. Serve very hot.

Serves 4

Bulgarian Beef Soup

½ lb. lean beef
4 large onions
3 tablespoons butter
½ teaspoon cumin seeds
mixed fresh herbs for small bouquet garni
6½ cups brown stock
salt and pepper
3 tablespoons sour cream
1 pint plain yogurt
1 tablespoon paprika
1 tablespoon cornstarch
¼ lb. cooked ham
sprigs parsley

1 Dice the beef finely. Peel the onions and cut into quarters.

2 Melt the butter in a big saucepan. Add the diced beef and onions, and sauté gently for 20 minutes, stirring frequently.

3 Put cumin seeds in a pepper mill and grind them. Wash and dry the herbs for the bouquet garni, and tie them together.

4 When the beef and onions have cooked for 20 minutes, add the brown stock and bouquet garni. Sprinkle with the ground cumin. Add salt and pepper, bearing in mind the seasoning of the stock, and cook for 20 minutes.

5 Put the sour cream into a bowl with the yogurt, paprika and cornstarch. Mix carefully so that lumps do not form, and pour into the soup. Stir with a wooden spoon over low heat.

6 Put the cooked ham through the grinder. Wash and dry the parsley sprigs and chop them finely.

7 Add the ham to the soup and cook a further 2 minutes over low heat.

8 Just before serving, remove the bouquet garni. Taste the soup, and if necessary adjust the seasoning. Pour it into a heated soup tureen, sprinkle with chopped parsley and serve hot.

Serves 6

Bulgarian Beef Soup is a nourishing and spicy meal in itself

Look 'n Cook Jumbo Shrimp Bisque

1 Ingredients for Jumbo Shrimp Bisque **2** For the sauce, make a roux with butter and flour, then blend in milk **3** Soften shrimp and vegetables in oil, add brandy and ignite. Add wine and tomatoes, season and cook **4** Take out shrimp, chop and return to pan **5** Press soup through conical strainer **6** Return to pan, boil, add remaining shrimp; place cream in tureen, pour in boiling soup (see opposite page) and serve

Fish Soups

Shrimp Bisque

4 tablespoons butter
$\frac{1}{4}$ cup flour
$4\frac{1}{4}$ cups milk
salt and pepper
5 tomatoes
1 shallot
1 small onion
1 branch celery
$\frac{1}{2}$ lb. unshelled jumbo shrimp
2 tablespoons oil
1 small bouquet garni
$\frac{1}{4}$ cup brandy
$\frac{1}{2}$ cup dry white wine

To finish:
2 peeled jumbo shrimp
$\frac{1}{2}$ cup heavy cream

1 Melt the butter in a double boiler and blend in the flour to make a roux. Cook for about 1 minute without letting it color. Using a wooden spoon, blend in the milk off the heat, then return to the stove and bring to a boil. Season with salt and pepper and cook for 20 minutes over low heat.

2 Skin the tomatoes and cut them in half. Remove the seeds and chop the pulp roughly. Peel and finely chop the shallot and onion. Wash and finely chop the celery.

3 Wash and dry the shrimp. Remove the heads and tails.

4 Heat the oil in a pan. When hot add the unshelled shrimp, the vege-tables (but not the tomatoes) and the bouquet garni. Cook gently for about 10 minutes or until the vegetables are soft.

5 Pour in the brandy, heat for about 1 minute, then ignite. When the flames die down, add the to-matoes and white wine. Add salt and season liberally with pepper, then cook for 20 minutes.

6 Remove the shrimp from the pan. Crush or chop them and put them back into the pan. Add the white sauce, mix and cook slowly for another 15 minutes. Heat a soup tureen.

7 Pour the soup through a fine conical strainer, pressing down well with a wooden spoon, back into the pan. Bring to a boil again, check the seasoning and add the peeled shrimp.

8 Pour the cream into the tureen, add the soup, while stirring vigorously, and serve.

Serves 4

Tip: The shrimp shells are used to add additional flavor to the soup. If unshelled shrimp are not available increase the weight of additional shrimp by about $\frac{1}{4}$ lb.

Cream of Mussel Soup

1¾ pints fresh mussels
2¼ cups dry white wine
2¼ cups water
pepper
1 bouquet garni
4 potatoes
2 carrots
1 onion
2 cloves
1½ lbs. cod fillets

For the thickening:
2 egg yolks
⅞ cup heavy cream
1 tablespoon cornstarch

1 Scrub and wash the mussels in several changes of water to ensure all the sand is removed. Put them in a large pan and add half the white wine and pepper to taste. Bring to a boil on high heat. Shake the pan from time to time until the mussels open.

2 Lift out the mussels, discarding any that stay closed; remove the shells. Pass the cooking juices through a fine piece of cheesecloth. Pour the juices back into the pan. Add the rest of the wine, the water and the bouquet garni. Bring to a boil.

3 Meanwhile, peel the potatoes and cut them into even pieces. Peel the carrots and cut them into thin slices. Peel the onion and stud it with the cloves. Add the carrots and onions only to the pan. Bring to a boil, then reduce the heat, cover and simmer for 20 minutes.

4 After 20 minutes' cooking, add the potatoes to the pan and cook for a further 25 minutes.

5 Put the egg yolks in a bowl, add the cream and cornstarch and mix with a fork.

6 Cut the fillets into small pieces and add to the pan; simmer for 5 minutes. Heat a soup tureen.

7 Pour a little of the hot soup into the egg yolk mixture. Blend well, then return it to the pan. Add the

mussels and reheat the soup gently for 2-3 minutes, without letting it come to a boil.

8 Take out the onion and the bouquet garni. Pour the soup into the tureen and serve hot.

Serves 4

Mock Caviar Soup

2 lbs. cod fillets
2 onions
4 cloves
3 cups fish stock
2¼ cups dry white wine
1 bay leaf
pinch white pepper
½ teaspoon salt

For the thickening:
¼ cup butter
2 egg yolks
2 tablespoons flour
1 cup heavy cream
¼ lb. lumpfish roe

1 Cut the fish fillets into small pieces. Peel the onions and stud 1 of them with the cloves.

2 Pour the stock and white wine into a large saucepan. Add the onions, bay leaf, pepper, salt and pieces of fish. Cover and as soon as it comes to a boil, reduce the heat and simmer for about 30 minutes.

3 Beat the butter to soften it. Then beat in the egg yolks, one at a time, and each time with half of the flour and the cream respectively.

4 Work the soup through a strainer or food mill, pressing the fish with a wooden spoon to extract all the juice. Pour this fish liquid back into the saucepan.

5 Blend a little of the hot fish liquid with the cream mixture in a bowl; then return it to the pan of soup. Reheat gently but do not boil and cook for about 15 minutes.

6 Heat a soup tureen. Pour in the

soup, add the lumpfish roe and stir. Taste and adjust the seasoning and serve at once.

Serves 4

Oyster Bisque

24 fresh large oysters
scant 1 cup water
2 medium onions
¼ cup butter
2 tablespoons flour
2½ cups milk
salt and pepper
¼ teaspoon paprika
2 tablespoons finely chopped
  parsley

1 Open the oysters, retain their juice but discard the shells. Soak the oysters in the water and their juice. Peel and finely chop the onions.

2 Heat 3 tablespoons butter in a pan. Add the onions and sauté slowly until they are just beginning to brown. Add the flour and stir with a wooden spoon for 3 minutes. Add one-third of the milk, stir again and cook for 2 minutes.

3 Drain the oysters, keeping the liquid in which they were soaked, and cut them into small pieces.

4 Mix the onion sauce with the rest of the milk and the soaking liquid in a double boiler. Season with salt and pepper to taste.

5 Add the oysters to the pan and leave 20 minutes over low heat, taking care the mixture does not boil. Add the chopped parsley.

6 Just before serving, stir in the rest of the butter and the paprika. Serve at once.

Serves 4

Cream of Mussel Soup — mussels, once considered the 'oysters of the poor,' are now featured in world-famous dishes. They are in season from March to September and should be bought alive. Test for freshness by sliding the two shells against each other — if they move they are probably full of sand or mud, not mussel

Sardine Soup

2 onions
2 leeks
1 small bunch fennel
2 tomatoes
5 cloves garlic
3 tablespoons olive oil
pinch saffron
1 bouquet garni
salt and pepper
2 small potatoes
8 large fresh sardines
2 slices bread

1 Peel and chop the onions. Clean and wash the leeks and fennel. Chop them finely. Bring a small pan of water to a boil. Dip the tomatoes in for a few seconds, drain them, put into cold water then peel and chop them. Peel and crush 4 cloves of garlic.

2 Pour the oil into a saucepan and gently sauté the onions, leeks and fennel in it on low heat for 10 minutes without them coloring. Then add the tomatoes and crushed garlic, the saffron and the bouquet garni. Add 4½ cups of water, salt and pepper and let it cook for 25 minutes with a lid on the pan.

3 Peel and wash the potatoes. Cut them into cubes and add them to the saucepan after it has been cooking for 15 minutes.

4 Clean the sardines. Rub them with a cloth to remove the scales. Remove the heads and rinse in clear water. Dry them and add them to the pan after the vegetables have been cooking for 25 minutes. Bring to a boil again and cook for a further 10 minutes.

5 Cut the remaining clove of garlic in two. Rub the slices of bread with it. Cut the bread in pieces, arrange them on the baking sheet and toast them under the broiler.

6 Warm up the soup tureen. Add the soup and take out the bouquet garni. Serve hot, with croûtons.

Serves 4

Sardine Soup is a rich, red soup with an inexpensive base

We normally associate sardines with the canned variety but larger, fresh sardines, which resemble herrings, are widely eaten around the Atlantic coasts. Strictly speaking, sardines are young pilchards but the term is also used for young herrings and sprats.

Pacific sardines are generally twice the size of the Atlantic kind. Anchovies are very small sardines and, when smoked, sardines are known as sprats. Sardines are mainly processed and canned in oil or tomato sauce but they can also be used fresh in many exciting and attractive dishes.

44

CHEF'S CHOICE

Fish Soups

Fish soups can be many things to many people, but two of the most famous are Bouillabaisse and Bourride from the Mediterranean. The fish, which is always removed from the broth for serving, is accompanied by toasted croûtons and a rich garlic mayonnaise — spicy rouille for the Bouillabaisse, and aioli for Bourride.
On the next page is a step-by-step guide to making Bouillabaisse

1 Wash and clean the fish; cut into pieces 2 Skin, seed and chop tomatoes; peel and finely chop onions, garlic and parsley; cut fennel and leeks into matchsticks 3 Sauté vegetables gently in oil 4 Add saffron, tomatoes, garlic and parsley 5 Add fish pieces 6 Strain broth and add to the pan 7 Pound together garlic, saf-

fron and cayenne for rouille **8** Blend in egg yolk and oil **9** Spread croûtes on baking sheet, pour over oil and bake **10** Season broth with salt and pepper as soon as it boils **11** Rub garlic over croûtes **12** Lift pieces of fish onto serving dish **13** Ladle some of the (continued on page 49)

Bouillabaisse started as a very simple fish soup made with spiny scorpion fish, olive oil, garlic, onion, leeks and sea water. It then evolved to its present form with the inclusion of many more different rock fish and flavorings, and in particular the special garlic mayonnaise called rouille.

Some rouille sauces can be very fiery, depending on the strength of the cayenne. And the blending of the hot broth with the sauce helps to thicken and bind it.

Sadly, it is difficult to reproduce this delicious dish exactly, away from the Mediterranean, mainly because the local fish are unobtainable, but the recipe here is an excellent alternative.

To be really tasty, Bouillabaisse must combine a wide variety of fish, each kind adding its own particular flavor. So 6 lbs. of fish is the smallest amount to use satisfactorily. The choice of fish is wide, the most popular being eel, bass, cod, halibut, snapper, haddock, together with shellfish like crab, lobster, or jumbo shrimp.

Bourride is another famous Mediterranean soup dish, but the classic recipe doesn't confine its choice of fish to rock sea fish as Bouillabaisse does. Often fatty fish, like sardines, are included and indeed in its earliest form, Bourride was a sardine soup bound with aioli, another kind of garlic mayonnaise.

hot broth over the pieces of fish
14 Pour the remaining broth into a hot soup tureen **15** Serve the platter of fish and shellfish separately from the rouille sauce, broth and croûtes

Bouillabaisse— Fish Soup Provençale

6 lbs. saltwater fish (use a variety of 6 or more kinds)
8-10 jumbo shrimp, fresh or frozen
few fish bones for stock
4 very ripe large tomatoes
4 large onions
1 carrot
1 bulb garlic (many cloves)
4 large leeks
2 bulbs fennel (not stalks)
1 cup olive oil
1 bouquet garni
pinch saffron
salt and pepper
1 large crusty loaf

For the rouille:
5 cloves garlic
salt
1 egg yolk
pinch cayenne pepper
pinch saffron
1¾ cups olive oil

1 Remove the skin and bones from the fish and wash them well. Roughly chop up the fish bones and wash them.

2 Cut the fish into pieces, making the slices from the more tender and delicate fish larger than the others. Wash them again. Clean the shrimp.

3 Peel, wash and dry the vegetables. Skin, deseed and chop the tomatoes. Peel the onions, carrot and garlic cloves; slice 1 onion and the carrot, then chop the remaining onions finely as well as a few cloves of garlic. Wash, dry and finely chop the parsley. Wash the leeks well, trim them and the fennel, then cut into fine matchsticks.

4 Heat 2-3 tablespoons of oil in a large pan. Sauté the sliced vegetables and chopped garlic in it on a very low heat for 2-3 minutes without letting them color, then add the chopped up fish bones. Cover liberally with cold water and add the bouquet garni. Bring to a boil, then simmer for 20 minutes on low heat. Skim the fish stock as necessary.

5 Peel 4 or 5 cloves of garlic and crush them.

6 Heat 3 tablespoons of oil in a large heavy pan. Add the chopped onions, fennel and leeks and fry gently for 3 or 4 minutes without letting them color. Then take them off the heat and sprinkle with the saffron. Mix well. Add the tomatoes and garlic and mix again.

7 Add the fish with the shrimp. Mix in carefully and let stand for about 30 minutes.

8 When the fish stock is cooked, pour it through a conical strainer and leave it to cool.

9 Pour the stock over the fish and other ingredients. If the liquid doesn't completely cover them add water to do so. Add salt and pepper, bring to a boil on high heat and simmer for 15 minutes. Check and adjust the seasoning halfway through the cooking.

10 During this time, prepare the rouille. Peel the garlic, chop it up very finely and put it in a mortar with an egg yolk, cayenne pepper, saffron and salt. Pound it well, then little by little incorporate the olive oil by trickling it in as when making mayonnaise, continuously stirring with the pestle instead of a wooden spoon. Then put the mixture in a sauceboat.

11 Cut the bread into slices and place on a baking sheet. Sprinkle with the rest of the olive oil and bake in a hot oven or toast under the broiler. Peel the rest of the garlic cloves. When the croûtes are ready rub them generously with the garlic. Heat a soup tureen.

12 Carefully put the fish and the shrimp onto a large serving dish, pour over them a ladle of stock and keep hot in the oven or under the broiler. Place the toasted croûtes in the hot soup tureen. Strain the stock into it. Serve at once with the rouille.

Serves 6–8

Bourride
(Fish Soup with Garlic Mayonnaise)

2 onions
2 firm, ripe tomatoes
4 cloves garlic
grated rind 1 orange
5 cups water
bunch fresh thyme, 2-3 fennel
  stalks and bay leaf
salt and pepper
pinch saffron
¼ cup olive oil
1¼ cups dry white wine
3 lbs. mixed sea fish (cod,
  haddock, flounder, red mullet)

1¼ cups aioli sauce (see right)
2 egg yolks
toasted croûtes of bread

1 Peel and chop the onions. Wash and chop the tomatoes. Peel and chop the garlic. Wash and dry the herbs. Bring the water to a boil.

2 Put the onions, tomatoes, garlic, grated orange rind and herbs in a large, heavy-based saucepan. Season with salt and pepper and add the saffron.

3 Stir the olive oil, followed by the white wine, into the onion mixture, then mix in the boiling water. Bring back to a boil.

4 Clean and wash the fish and cut into chunks if very large. Add them to the pan of boiling broth and cook for 10 minutes. Then lift the fish out of the pan, using a slotted spoon, and keep hot.

5 Strain the fish broth through a fine strainer; either rub through the vegetables at the same time or purée in a blender and return to the broth; reheat. Heat a soup tureen.

6 Beat the egg yolks and blend with half the aioli in a bowl. Gradually add a ladleful of the boiling broth and blend together; return this mixture to the pot of soup, stir in and reheat gently but do not boil.

7 Put the toasted croûtes of bread in the bottom of a hot soup tureen and pour in the soup. Serve at once, with the dish of fish separately, and accompanied by the rest of the aioli in a sauceboat.

Serves 6

Aioli
(Garlic Mayonnaise)

6 garlic cloves
1 cup olive oil
2 egg yolks
salt and pepper
½ lemon

1 Peel the cloves of garlic, put them in a mortar and pestle and pound, while gradually adding about 1 tablespoon of the oil, until they are reduced to a paste.

2 Add the egg yolks to the garlic paste in the mortar and mix well with a wooden spoon. Then add the remaining oil, little by little, stirring continuously at the same time. Add salt and pepper to taste.

3 When the mayonnaise has thickened, squeeze the juice from the lemon, strain and stir into the mayonnaise. Cover and chill until required.

Makes about 1¼ cups

Bourride

Appetizers

These can be either a single ingredient or two, simply served, like Parma (prosciutto) ham with figs or melon, or several combined together, like Seafood Hors d'Oeuvre or Stuffed Artichokes. Ideally, appetizers should stimulate the appetite, not dull it, so choose ingredients that contrast well in flavor, texture and color, and only serve small portions

Cold Appetizers

Tomatoes Stuffed with Cream and Herbs

4 large round firm tomatoes
bunch mixed fresh herbs (chervil, tarragon, chives, etc.)
2 shallots
1 clove garlic
6 tablespoons heavy cream
salt and pepper
few lettuce leaves

1 Scoop out the tomatoes (see opposite page). Wash, dry and chop the herbs finely. Peel and chop the shallots and garlic.

2 Rinse and dry the tomato shells. Whip the cream until fairly stiff, then fold in the herbs, shallots, garlic, salt and pepper. Fill the tomatoes with this mixture and put a lid on each one. Chill until ready to serve.

3 Wash and dry the lettuce leaves, then arrange on a serving dish. Arrange the stuffed tomatoes on the dish and serve.

Serves 4

Swedish Herring Rissoles

3 medium potatoes
2 onions
2 tablespoons butter
3 fresh herring (skinned and filleted)
salt and pepper
nutmeg
1 cup red currant jelly
½ cup oil

1 Wash the potatoes without peeling them, and cook them in salted boiling water. Peel and finely chop the onions.

2 Melt the butter in a pan, and cook the onions, without letting them color too much, for 7 or 8 minutes. Put them to one side and leave to cool.

Tomatoes Stuffed with Cream and Herbs are simple to prepare and make a light, refreshing start to any meal

3 When the potatoes are cooked, cool them in cold water, then peel them and mash them to a purée.

4 Put the herring fillets through the grinder. Add the onions, potatoes, a little salt, pepper and a little grated nutmeg. Mix well together, then shape into round flat rissoles.

5 Put the red currant jelly and ⅔ cup water in a saucepan and heat slowly.

6 Heat the oil in a skillet. When it is hot, cook the rissoles for about 10 minutes, turning them over once or twice.

7 Heat a serving dish and a sauceboat.

8 Arrange the rissoles on the dish. Pour the hot red currant jelly sauce into the sauceboat and serve very hot.

Serves 4

Tip: The mixture of sweet and savory is typical of Scandinavian cookery. Ascertain the tastes of guests before serving this recipe or leave out the sauce.

Herring in Sherry Pickle

2 salted herring, filleted and skinned
⅓ cup sherry
¼ cup water
3 tablespoons wine vinegar
¼ teaspoon allspice
2 onions, thinly sliced into rings
chopped fresh dill

1 Cover the herring with cold water and leave to soak for 24 hours. Drain, rinse and dry. Place in a non-metallic bowl.

2 Combine the sherry, water, vinegar and allspice. Pour over the herring. Cover with plastic wrap and refrigerate for 24 hours.

3 Serve garnished with the onion rings and dill.

Serves 4

Look 'n Cook Scooping out Tomatoes

1 and **2** Cut out tomato stalk end, then cut a slice from the other end to give a flat base; use as a lid **3** Using a melon baller or teaspoon, scoop out seeds and core, leaving sides and base intact **4** Sprinkle insides with salt to draw out moisture, turn upside down, drain, dry and then stuff

Seafood Hors D'Oeuvre

pinch sea salt
1 onion
bay leaf
bouquet garni
4½ cups mussels
1 can crab
1 small can tomato paste
1 tablespoon brandy
scant 1 cup heavy cream
salt and pepper
1 lb. fresh or frozen shrimp
small bunch parsley

1 Peel the onion and cut in slices.

2 Prepare the cooking liquid (court bouillon): in a large saucepan put 1¼ cups water, the onion, the bay leaf and the bouquet garni; simmer for 20 minutes.

3 Scrape the mussels and wash them in several changes of water. Put the shellfish in the court bouillon and cook gently, stirring now and then, until they open. Discard any which do not open.

4 When the mussels are fully open, lift them out of the saucepan with a skimming ladle. Shell them and put in a dish.

5 Put the liquid through a strainer lined with a fine cloth and set it aside.

6 Open the can of crab, drain it, remove any cartilage and quickly flake the flesh.

7 Open the can of tomato paste. Pour the contents into a bowl. Stir in the brandy, then pour in the cream, stirring constantly, as though thickening mayonnaise. Then add 5 tablespoons of the reserved seafood liquid and mix. Add a little salt and a generous sprinkling of pepper. The sauce should now be well seasoned and very smooth.

8 Divide the mussels, flaked crab and peeled shrimp among 8 individual serving dishes and pour sauce over each.

9 Wash, dry and chop the parsley. Sprinkle some on top of each dish.

10 Refrigerate and serve chilled.

Serves 8

Crunchy Salad Starter

1 small head white cabbage
coarse salt
salt and pepper
⅔ packed cup golden raisins
½ branch celery
2 apples
juice ½ lemon
1 teaspoon prepared mustard
1 tablespoon vinegar
3 tablespoons olive oil
1 cup chopped walnuts

1 Trim the cabbage, pulling off any withered leaves, the hard core and side leaves. Wash the remainder. Dry and shred them finely with a large kitchen knife. Sprinkle with coarse salt and leave for about 30 minutes to draw out excess moisture.

2 Soak the raisins in warm water for 10 minutes.

3 Clean the celery. Wash, dry and dice it. Peel and core the apples, then dice, sprinkle with lemon juice.

4 Drain the shredded cabbage, dry it on absorbent paper and put into a salad bowl with the celery. Mix well.

5 Make a dressing by blending together the mustard, vinegar and oil, season with salt and pepper and stir well. Pour this over the cabbage and celery and mix well but do not crush the ingredients.

6 Drain and dry the raisins and add them to the bowl, together with the nuts and diced apple. Stir again and serve immediately.

Serves 6

Ham Logs

6 thick slices very lean ham
1½ small celery hearts
2 shallots
handful parsley
small bunch chives
juice ½ lemon
3 ozs. cream cheese
1 teaspoon strong mustard
salt
1 teaspoon paprika
pinch cayenne pepper
1 cup chopped walnuts

1 Cut 2 of the slices of ham into fine strips.

2 Clean the celery and chop it as finely as possible. Peel and finely chop the shallots. Wash, dry and chop the parsley and chives.

3 Mash the cheese and beat in the parsley, chives, shallots, 1 tablespoon lemon juice, the mustard, salt, paprika and cayenne pepper.

4 Stir in the chopped ham, celery and nuts. Beat well until the mixture is very smooth and creamy. Spread this mixture on the four remaining ham slices and roll these up to form 'logs.' Serve chilled, on a bed of lettuce and decorated with sliced tomatoes and a few sprigs of parsley.

Serves 4

Seafood Hors d'Oeuvre is a delicious medley of shellfish, brandy and cream

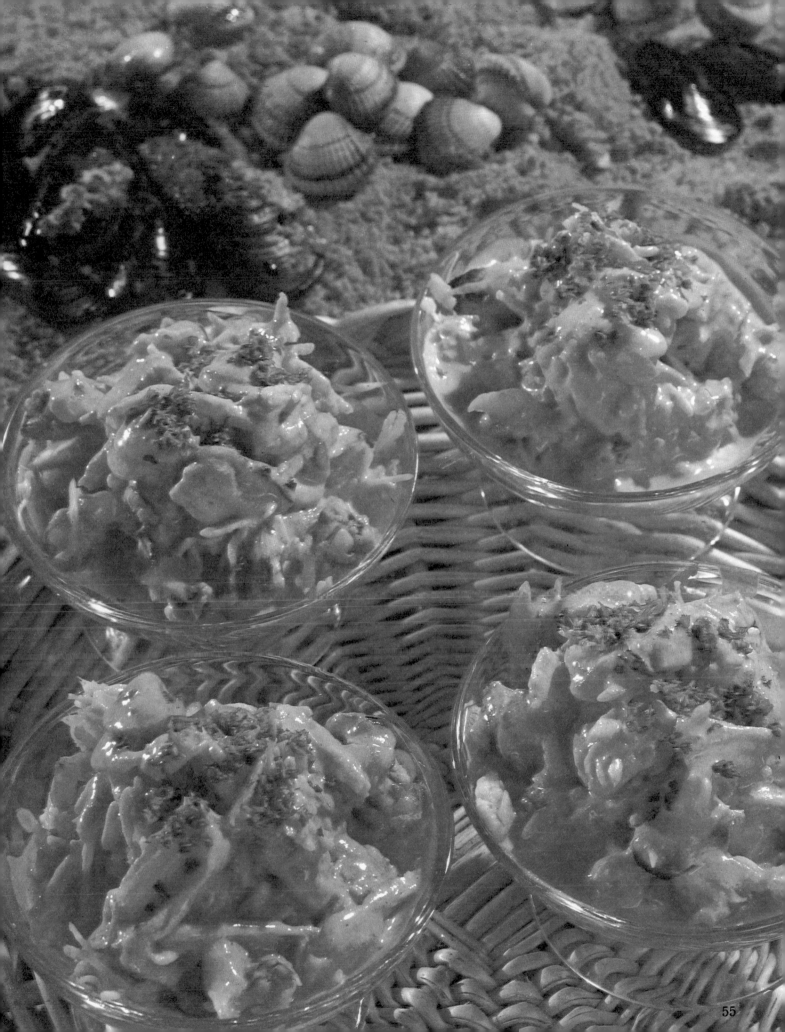

Artichoke Hearts with Cottage Cheese

1½ cups cottage cheese
4 large globe artichokes
large bunch chives, chervil and
  parsley, mixed
salt and pepper
pinch cayenne pepper
few lettuce leaves

For the Blanching Mixture:
juice 3 lemons
1 tablespoon flour
6⅓ cups water

1 Put the cottage cheese in a cloth-lined strainer and leave to drain completely.

2 Prepare the artichoke hearts and blanch (see pages 58–59). Cook them for 40 minutes in the blanching mixture, or till tender, then drain and cool.

3 Wash the herbs; dry them well and chop finely. Put them into a bowl. Add the cottage cheese, salt and pepper, and cayenne, and mix well with a fork; then beat vigorously.

4 Wash and dry the lettuce leaves. Arrange them on a serving dish. Lay the artichoke hearts on the lettuce and pile a pyramid of the cheese mixture on each one. Serve chilled.

Serves 4

Apple Hors d'Oeuvre

1 lemon
1 small celery heart
1 small cucumber
few lettuce leaves
3 tomatoes
few sprigs chives and chervil
¾ cup heavy cream
½ teaspoon paprika
salt and pepper
3 eating apples
12 radishes

1 Squeeze the lemon and reserve the juice. Wash the celery and chop it into fine strips.

2 Peel the cucumber, split it in half lengthwise and remove the seeds. Sprinkle both halves with salt, to remove the excess moisture.

3 Wash and dry the lettuce leaves. Wash and dry the tomatoes and then quarter them. Wash the chives and the chervil; dry and chop them.

4 In a bowl beat together the cream, lemon juice and paprika, and season with salt and pepper.

5 Rinse and dry the cucumber and cut it into small cubes. Peel and core the apples and dice them.

6 Put the cucumber, apples, celery and tomatoes into a dish. Pour the cream sauce over and stir it in.

7 Wash and scrape the radishes. Cut them into flower shapes.

8 Line the sides and bottom of a salad bowl with the lettuce leaves. Arrange the salad in the center. Sprinkle with the chopped chives and chervil, and decorate with the radishes. Serve chilled.

Serves 6

Apple Hors d'Oeuvre is a refreshing starter which sharpens the taste buds

Finnish Pickled Herring

  ★ ☒☒☒

4 salted herring, filleted and
  skinned
4 small onions
1 carrot
1¾ cups wine vinegar
1 cup water
½ cup sugar
3 bay leaves
2 inches gingerroot, sliced thinly
2 teaspoons mustard seed
1 tablespoon prepared horseradish

1 Soak herring in cold water for at least 24 hours. Rinse, drain and dry, Cut into ½-inch strips. Peel and thinly slice the onions and carrot.

2 Put the vinegar, water and sugar into a pan and bring to a boil over moderate heat. Simmer for about 5 minutes until syrupy.

3 In a non-metallic bowl arrange in this order, herring, bay leaves, gingerroot, mustard seed, horseradish, sliced onion and carrot. Pour the vinegar syrup over the fish.

4 Cover with plastic wrap and refrigerate for 3 days.

5 Drain and serve with some of the onion slices.

Serves 4

Scandinavian Hors d'Oeuvre

 ★ ☒

½ small head red cabbage
½ small head white cabbage
coarse salt and pepper
6 herring, marinated in vinegar
2 mild onions
3 cooking apples
few green fennel leaves (fresh)
1 teaspoon prepared mustard
2 tablespoons vinegar
5 tablespoons olive oil
1 teaspoon cumin seeds
¼ cup heavy cream

1 Clean the cabbages. Remove the hard cores and any withered leaves. Wash and dry them, then shred with a large kitchen knife.

2 Put the red and white cabbages into separate bowls, sprinkle with coarse salt and let stand for 30 minutes (this removes excess moisture).

3 During this time, drain the herrings and fillet them.

4 Peel the onions, cut them into thin slices, and separate into rings. Peel the apples, cut them in quarters and remove the core and seeds, then dice the fruit. Wash, dry and chop the fennel.

5 Mix the mustard, vinegar and oil in a bowl and pepper lightly.

6 Drain both red and white cabbages. Dry them with a cloth and put them into two bowls. Add half the diced apple to each one. Season with the mustard vinaigrette sauce.

7 Arrange the herring fillets in the bottom of a serving dish. Sprinkle them with cumin seeds, cover with the onion rings, coat with cream and then sprinkle with chopped fennel.

8 Surround the herring fillets with the two cabbage salads and serve cold.

Serves 6

Scandinavian Hors d'Oeuvre is a crunchy, summer starter with herring marinated in vinegar

Look 'n Cook Preparation of Artichoke Hearts

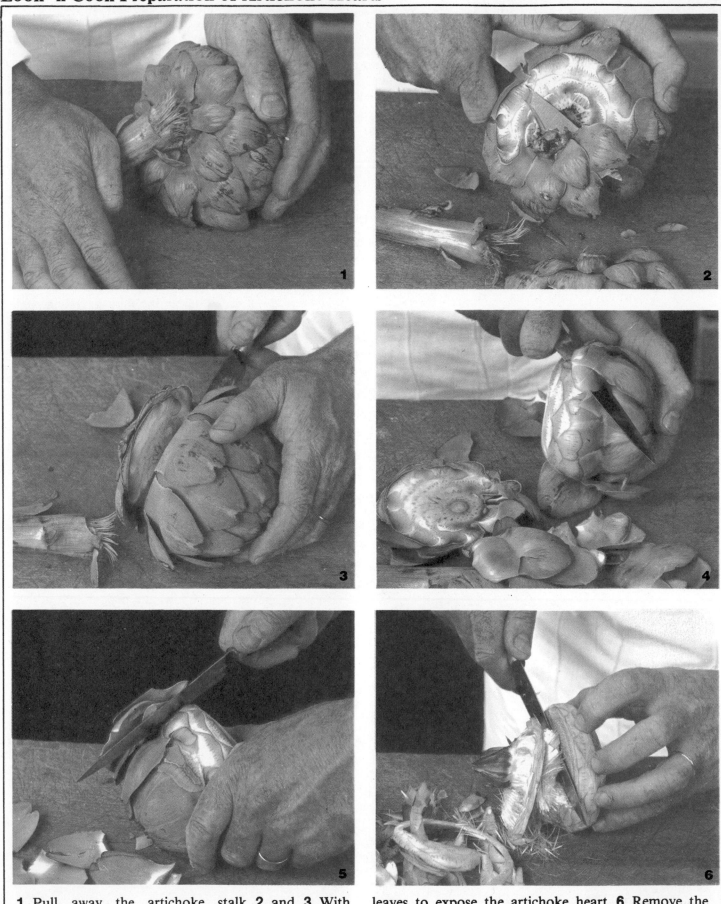

1 Pull away the artichoke stalk **2** and **3** With scissors snip off the tips of the leaves, then cut around and level the base **4** and **5** Cut away remaining leaves to expose the artichoke heart **6** Remove the 'hairy' center (choke) **7** Trim around the heart to neaten **8** and **9** Rub a cut lemon over each heart to

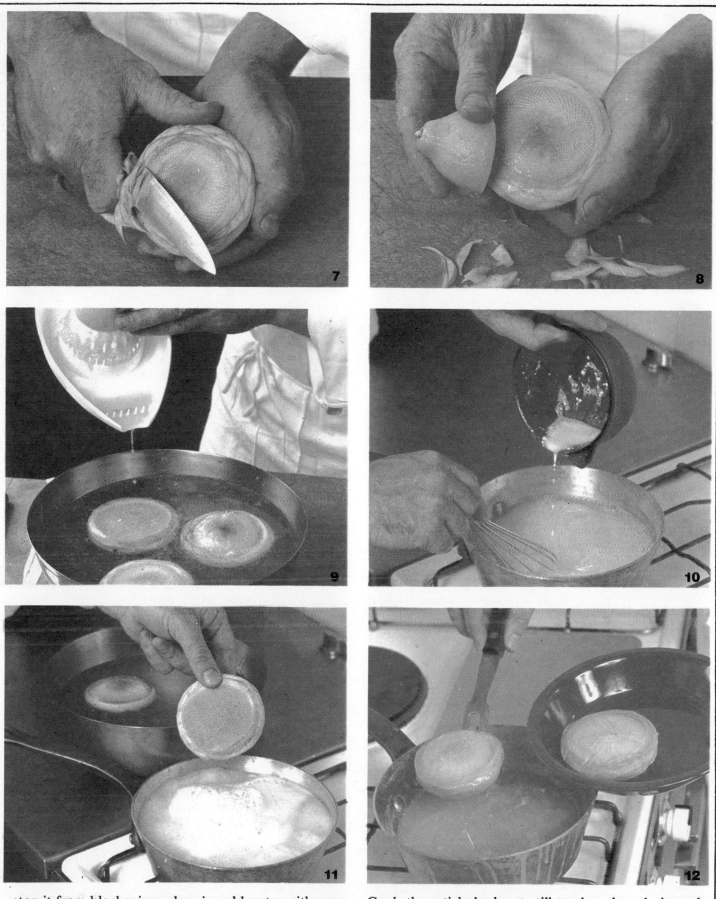

stop it from blackening; place in cold water with some of the lemon juice **10** Mix flour with remaining lemon juice and whisk into boiling salted water **11** and **12**

Cook the artichoke hearts till tender, then drain and chill them until needed

Cucumber Boats with Yogurt

1 large cucumber
salt and pepper
1 small bunch chives
4 large lettuce leaves
1 cup plain yogurt
½ cup cottage cheese

1 Skin the cucumber, cut into half lengthwise and take the seeds out with a small spoon. Then cut each half in two to make 4 even-sized shells or boats. Sprinkle them with salt to draw out the excess moisture and leave to drain upside down in a strainer.

2 Dry the cucumber boats on absorbent paper. Wash, dry and chop the chives. Wash and dry the lettuce leaves and use to garnish a serving dish.

3 Put the yogurt, cottage cheese, chives, salt and pepper into a bowl and mix well. Fill the cucumber boats with the mixture, arrange them on the serving dish and serve very cold.

Serves 4

Stuffed Artichokes Mimosa

The term 'mimosa' is used for any dish finished with a sprinkling of strained hard-boiled egg yolk, and is derived from its close resemblance to tiny yellow mimosa flowers.

4 globe artichokes
1 egg plus 1 egg yolk
salt and pepper
1 teaspoon prepared mustard
1 cup olive oil
1½ cups shelled shrimp
few lettuce leaves
1 small bunch parsley
8 jumbo shrimp

For the Blanching Mixture:
juice 3 lemons
1 tablespoon flour
6⅓ cups water

1 Prepare the artichoke hearts and blanch (see pages 58–59). Cook them for 40 minutes in the blanching mixture, or till tender, then drain and cool.

2 Hard-boil the egg, cool in cold water and then shell. Cut in half and scoop out the egg yolk; set aside.

3 Put the raw egg yolk in a bowl. Add salt and pepper and the mustard. Mix together, then beat in the oil in a steady stream, beating all the time. When all the oil has been incorporated, add the lemon juice and mix again. Add the shelled shrimp to the mayonnaise and chill in the refrigerator.

4 Wash and dry the lettuce leaves, then arrange them on a serving dish. Wash and dry the parsley and chop it finely.

5 Put the artichoke hearts on the lettuce leaves and fill with the shrimp mayonnaise. Rub the hard-boiled egg yolk through a strainer over the artichoke hearts. Sprinkle over the chopped parsley and garnish with the shrimp. Serve very cold.

Serves 4

Tip: If liked, vary the shrimp mayonnaise by adding a pinch of cayenne or 1 tablespoon tomato catsup.

Ham with Figs

8 well ripened fresh figs
4 slices cured or cooked ham

1 Peel the figs and cut them into halves.

2 Roll the slices of ham like ice cream cones and put a fig in each.

3 Arrange the ham rolls in a star

pattern on a dish, and arrange the remainder of the opened figs interspersed between them.

4 Serve cold.

Serves 4

Zakouski — Russian Hors d'Oeuvre

2 marinated herring
2½ lemons
2 tablespoons heavy cream
fresh green fennel leaves
4 dill pickles
½ lb. thin slices smoked eel
½ lb. thin slices smoked salmon
fish roe as available — grey caviar, salmon eggs or lumpfish roe
thin slices rye bread
½ cup sweet butter

1 Drain the marinated herring and fillet them. Then make a purée by putting the herring in a blender or through a grinder. Squeeze the half lemon and mix the lemon juice and cream with the herring purée.

2 Arrange the herring purée in a glass dish. Wash and dry the fennel leaves, chop them and sprinkle over the herring purée.

3 Surrounding the purée, arrange the dill pickles and thinly sliced smoked fish of various kinds in separate dishes. Put the fish roe in the center. If serving caviar, place it in a dish of crushed ice. Serve rye bread, butter and the remaining lemons, cut in quarters, with the zakouski.

Serves 4

Tip: If wished, supplement the zakouski with a dish of 'crudités' — radish roses, fresh cucumber peeled and cut into about 3-inch chunks, scallions, tiny firm tomatoes, etc.

Zakouski — a Russian hors d'oeuvre

Anchovy and Garlic Stuffed Eggs make and attractive egg starter.

Oyster Cocktails

2 dozen fresh oysters
2 small celery branches
$\frac{1}{4}$ cup tomato catsup
$\frac{1}{3}$ cup gin
1 tablespoon cream
1 teaspoon lemon juice
salt and pepper
pinch cayenne pepper
bunch chervil
1 teaspoon paprika

1 Open the oysters with an oyster knife and scape them from the shells. Drain them, keeping the juice. Strain the juice through cheesecloth and put the oysters in a bowl.

2 Wash and dry the celery branches. Chop them finely and add to the oysters.

3 Stir into the oyster liquor the tomato catsup, gin, cream and lemon juice and beat for a moment. Taste and adjust the seasoning. Then add a pinch of cayenne pepper.

4 Pour this sauce over the oysters and celery and mix gently. Spoon the oyster cocktail into 4 glasses or small bowls.

5 Wash, dry and chop the chervil.

Sprinkle the chopped chervil over the cocktails together with some paprika. Chill the glasses or bowls in the refrigerator for 1 hour and serve very cold.

Serves 4

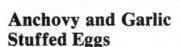

Anchovy and Garlic Stuffed Eggs

4 eggs
4 large cloves garlic
3 tablespoons butter
salt and pepper
8 olives
8 anchovy fillets
few lettuce leaves
chopped parsley
4 small tomatoes

1 Put the eggs in a pan of cold water and bring to a boil. Peel the garlic cloves and add to the boiling water. Remove them after 7 minutes, drain and then pound in a mortar.

2 When the water has been boiling for 10 minutes, take out the eggs, cool them in cold water and shell. Cut the shelled hard-boiled eggs in half lengthwise. Leave them to cool.

3 Put the butter in a bowl and work it to a very soft paste with a wooden spoon.

4 Carefully remove the yolks from the eggs, without damaging the whites. Mash and sieve the yolks, and add them to the softened butter. Then add the garlic purée and stir well until smooth. Season.

5 Pile this paste back into the half egg whites. Decorate each with an olive with an anchovy fillet wrapped around it.

6 Arrange the lettuce leaves on a serving platter, place the stuffed eggs on top and sprinkle with the finely-chopped parsley. Slice the tomatoes in half horizontally and use the halves to garnish the platter. Refrigerate and serve cold.

Serves 4

Smoked Fish Starter

1 head white cabbage (small)
2 marinated herring
½ teaspoon cumin seed
6 tablespoons heavy cream
3 smoked sprats or brisling
  sardines
2 lemons
2 apples
12 thin slices whole wheat bread
¼ cup butter
½ lb. thin slices smoked salmon
6 thin slices smoked eel
coarse salt and pepper

1 Trim, wash and dry the cabbage and shred it finely with a large sharp kitchen knife. Put the shredded cabbage into a bowl, sprinkle lightly with salt and leave to stand while continuing with the preparation.

2 Drain the marinated herring and fillet them. Put the fillets in a blender or through a grinder to make a purée. Add to this half the cumin and 2 tablespoons cream.

3 Wash the smoked sprats

4 Squeeze 1 lemon and reserve juice. Wash and dry the second lemon and cut it in thin rounds, then each round in half.

5 Peel the apples and cut them in quarters, remove the cores and seeds and dice.

6 Butter 9 slices of whole wheat bread and cut them diagonally to make 18 triangles. Arrange the slices of smoked eel on 6 of these triangles, and the slices of smoked salmon on the others. Pipe around a border of mayonnaise if liked.

7 Butter the remainder of the slices of bread with the herring purée, and cut them into triangles. Place 1 fillet on each of the triangles, and a semicircle of lemon on each slice.

8 Drain and dry the cabbage. Add to it the diced apple and the rest of the cumin. Sprinkle with lemon juice and pepper and mix gently.

9 Arrange the cabbage in a heap in the center of a serving dish, and pour on the rest of the cream. Arrange the various fish-covered triangles of bread around the edge of the dish and serve cold.

Serves 6

An eye-catching appetizer, choose several kinds of smoked fish for color and flavor contrast

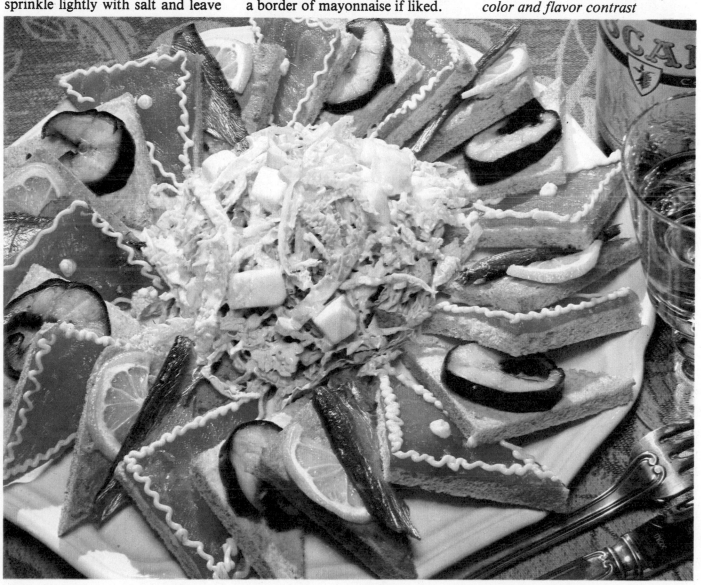

Tuna Fish with Eggplant in Sweet-sour Sauce (Caponata)

In Sicily this dish is a speciality and is called Caponata; some versions omit the tuna fish.

3 eggplants
1 small branch celery
4¼ cups water
6 canned anchovies, drained
5 large ripe firm tomatoes
1 large onion
1 bunch parsley
½ cup olive oil
salt and pepper
few sprigs thyme
1 bay leaf
1½ tablespoons sugar
2 teaspoons vinegar
1 cup small black olives
3 tablespoons capers
1½ cups canned tuna

1 Peel the eggplants. Cut them into cubes, sprinkle with salt to draw out the excess moisture and any bitterness and leave for about 30 minutes. Wash and trim the celery, and slice thinly.

2 Bring the water to a boil, add salt and put in the celery; simmer for about 8 minutes, then drain and plunge into a pan of cold water; drain again and set aside.

3 Wash the anchovies to remove the excess salt. Separate the fillets and rinse again thoroughly in water. Cut them into small pieces.

4 Skin the tomatoes; quarter them, remove the seeds and chop the flesh. Peel and thinly slice the onion. Wash, dry and chop the parsley.

5 Heat 2 tablespoons oil in a saucepan. When hot, add the onion and cook gently until soft but not browned. Add the tomatoes, season with salt and pepper, add the thyme and bay leaf and cook over very low heat until the mixture is a soft pulp. Remove the thyme and bay leaf and rub the mixture through a conical strainer.

6 Put the tomato purée in a pan, add the sugar and cook until thickened and lightly browned. Then add the vinegar and cook for a further 3-4 minutes.

7 Meanwhile, drain and dry the eggplant pieces. Heat the rest of the oil in a saucepan, put in the eggplant and cook briskly until lightly browned. Drain off the oil.

8 Remove the pan of tomato sauce from the heat and stir into the eggplants, together with the celery, anchovies, black olives and capers. Correct the seasoning — this dish should be fairly spicy — and mix together.

9 Set the mixture aside to cool, then chill in the refrigerator overnight. Turn the mixture into a salad bowl. Break the tuna fish into regular bite-size pieces and arrange over the top. Chill and serve.

Serves 6

Tuna fish and eggplant in a piquant sauce, a deliciously refreshing dish for a hot summer's day

Cold Appetizers

Mussels in Spicy Sauce

1 cup canned or bottled mussels, drained
2 tablespoons mayonnaise
2 teaspoons mustard
1 teaspoon sherry
½ teaspoon lemon juice
2 small bottled or canned pimentos

1 Put the mussels in the serving dish.

2 To the mayonnaise add the mustard, sherry and lemon juice and stir carefully until blended. Cut the pimentos into strips and stir into the sauce.

3 Spoon this sauce over the mussels.

Serves 2

Tip: This is a tasty way of serving mussels when fresh ones are not in season.

If using fresh, reserve a few shells for decoration.

Cauliflower in Vinegar

1 medium cauliflower
salt
1 cup vinegar
1 cup water
1 clove garlic, cut in half
2 teaspoons dried basil
3 tablespoons olive oil
1 tablespoon lime or lemon juice
1 teaspoon chopped parsley
1 teaspoon chopped chives
freshly ground black pepper

1 Wash and trim the cauliflower and divide into florets or sprigs. Add to boiling salted water and cook for 10-15 minutes. Drain.

2 Bring the vinegar, water, garlic and basil to a boil and pour over the cauliflower. Leave until cold, then chill.

3 Mix the oil, lime or lemon juice, parsley, chives, salt and black pepper to make a smooth dressing. Drain the cauliflower, pour on the dressing and serve at once.

Serves 6

Red Peppers and Mushrooms

½ lb. mushrooms
salt and pepper
2 lemons
5 tablespoons olive oil
6 large red peppers
small bunch chervil

1 Clean the mushrooms. Cut the ends off the stalks. Wash the mushrooms quickly but do not leave them underwater longer than necessary. Slice them thinly and season with salt and pepper.

2 Squeeze 1 of the lemons and sprinkle 2 tablespoons of the juice and 2 tablespoons olive oil over the mushrooms. Leave them to marinate.

3 Wash and dry the peppers. Broil them under high heat (the skin should swell and darken) or hold over a flame on a skewer. Then rinse them under cold water and peel them. The darkened outer skin should come off very easily, exposing the soft red flesh underneath.

4 Cut the peppers in half and remove the seeds. Cut the flesh in strips. Season with salt and pepper, and sprinkle on the rest of the lemon juice and oil.

5 Wash the other lemon and quarter it. Wash, dry and chop the chervil.

6 Mix the peppers and mushrooms together in a deep dish. Garnish with the lemon quarters and sprinkle chervil over the top. Chill 1 hour before serving.

Serves 6

Red Herring with Sauerkraut

6 herring fillets (smoked and salted)
3 tablespoons olive oil
2 sweet eating apples
1 lb. sauerkraut
2 mild onions
1 lemon
2 tablespoons heavy cream
1 cup plain yogurt
pepper
bunch parsley

1 Cut the herring fillets into small pieces. Put them on a deep plate and pour the oil over them.

2 Peel, core and dice the apples.

3 Wash the sauerkraut in fresh water. Drain it thoroughly, squeezing with the hands to extract all the water. Put it into a cloth, dry it well, then separate the shreds.

4 Peel the onions. Cut them into rounds, then separate into rings. Squeeze the juice from the lemon.

5 Mix the lemon juice with the cream and yogurt. Add pepper to taste and blend all these ingredients together.

6 Mix the sauerkraut and the diced apple, pour on the lemon-flavored yogurt and stir gently.

7 Wash, dry and chop the parsley.

8 Arrange the sauerkraut and apple salad around the edge of a serving dish.

9 Drain the herring fillets and place them in the center of the dish. Cover them with the onion rings. Sprinkle with chopped parsley and serve very cold.

Serves 6

Vegetables à la Grecque

3 globe artichoke hearts
1 small cauliflower
1 lemon
½ lb. mushrooms
3 carrots
2 bulbs fennel
3 turnips
2 leeks
3 cloves garlic
½ lb. green olives
1 cup olive oil
1 tablespoon tomato paste
1 teaspoon coriander seeds
½ cup wine vinegar
salt and pepper

1 Peel and wash all the vegetables. Break the cauliflower into florets. Squeeze the juice of the lemon.

2 Put the artichoke hearts, the cauliflower florets, the mushrooms (whole small ones, cut in half if large) into water. Add the lemon juice to prevent the vegetables from discoloring.

3 Slice the carrots, fennel, turnips and leeks. Peel and crush the garlic. Pit the olives and wash in cold water.

4 Heat the oil in a pan. When it is hot, add the leeks, then all the other vegetables, stirring all the time to prevent them from sticking.

5 Add the crushed garlic, the tomato paste, the coriander, the vinegar, the water, salt and pepper.

6 Cook for 12–15 minutes, stirring from time to time. The vegetables should stay firm. When cooked, let cool.

Serves 8–10

Artichokes à la Grecque

4 globe artichokes
2 lemons
½ lb. canned tomatoes, drained

6 shallots
½ cup olive oil
6 coriander seeds
1 bouquet garni
½ cup dry white wine
salt and pepper

1 Prepare the artichoke hearts (see page 58). Cut 1 lemon in half. Rub the artichoke hearts with one half. Squeeze the other half, pouring the juice into a bowl. Fill the bowl with water.

2 Cut the hearts into 4 or 6 pieces. Remove all the hairs with a serrated knife. Dip the artichokes into the lemon water.

3 Put the artichokes into a saucepan. Add the lemon water. Bring to a boil and boil for 1 minute. Chop the tomatoes roughly. Peel the shallots and squeeze the last lemon.

4 Warm the oil in a sauté pan. Drain the artichokes and put them into the pan. Add the tomatoes, the shallots, the coriander seeds, the bouquet garni, the lemon juice and the white wine. Add seasoning, cover and cook on low heat for 30 minutes.

5 When the cooking is finished, remove the bouquet garni, put the artichoke pieces into an hors d'oeuvre dish. Leave to cool, then put the dish in the refrigerator.

Serves 4

Vegetables à la Grecque — mixed vegetables served cold in this way make a delicious starter

Look 'n Cook Artichoke Hearts à la Grecque

1 Cut the hearts into pieces and put into lemon water **2** Cut away the hairy part **3** Put the hearts into a pan, strain the lemon water over them and boil for 1 minute **4** The ingredients **5** Put all the ingredients into a sauté pan and cook gently **6** The finished dish. Keep in the refrigerator until needed.

Parma Ham with Melon

1 medium ripe honeydew or
  cantaloupe
¼ lb. prosciutto (Parma ham)
freshly ground black pepper

1 Cut the melon into halves, scoop out the seeds and, if liked, peel. Cut into 4-6 portions.

2 Put onto individual plates. Lay rolls of the paper-thin ham across each portion. Cover with plastic wrap to prevent the ham from drying out and chill for 30 minutes before serving.

4 Pass the pepper mill at the table or serve with freshly ground black pepper.

Serves 4–6

Cantaloupe Hors d'Oeuvre

3 small cantaloupes
6 tablespoons white port
½ lb. prosciutto (Parma ham)
  sliced wafer-thin

1 Chill the melons for a few hours before beginning the preparation.

2 Halve the melons horizontally to give 6 cup-shaped pieces. Scoop out the seeds and drain off excess juices.

3 With a melon baller, scoop little balls from the flesh of the melons. Replace these balls in the melon cups. Sprinkle port over each cup.

4 Lightly roll the thin slices of ham and pile them on top of the melon halves. Serve chilled.

Serves 6

Tip: If small melons are not available use larger ones and cut the halves into 2 or 3 sections each after step 2 above.

Avocado Stuffed with Tuna Fish

3 medium-large avocados
juice 1 lemon
6½ ozs. canned tuna
1-2 cloves garlic
1 small onion
2 teaspoons capers
salt and freshly ground black
  pepper

For the garnish:
1 small onion
stuffed olives
lettuce leaves

1 Cut the avocados in half lengthwise and remove the pits. Dip all the exposed surfaces in lemon juice to prevent discoloring.

2 Peel and crush the garlic; peel and finely chop 1 onion, thinly slice the other. Flake the tuna fish and mix it with the garlic, chopped onion, capers, salt and pepper.

3 Pile the mixture onto the avocado halves, and garnish with sliced onion and stuffed olives. Put lettuce leaves on individual plates, stand an avocado on each and chill 30 minutes before serving.

Serves 6

Watercress and Walnut Salad

3 eggs
bunch watercress
⅓ cup white vinegar
12 shelled walnuts
¼ cup cubed Gruyère cheese
1 apple
2 shallots
1 tablespoon white mustard
¼ cup olive oil
salt and pepper

1 Place the eggs in a saucepan. Cover with cold water, add a little salt, bring to a boil and continue boiling for 10 minutes.

2 Prepare the cress: keeping only the green leaves and tender stalks, wash them very thoroughly in several changes of water. Soak the cress in cold water with half the vinegar added.

3 Run cold water over the hard-boiled eggs. Shell and quarter them.

4 Peel the apple. Quarter it, remove the core and slice thinly. Peel the shallots and chop them finely.

5 Drain the cress and rinse in clean water; drain carefully. Place in a salad bowl. Add the sliced apple, quartered walnuts and cheese.

6 Make a dressing by mixing in a cup the remaining vinegar, the mustard, oil, shallots, salt and pepper. Pour this dressing over the salad and mix it in. Decorate the salad with the egg quarters and the nut pieces. Serve at once.

Serves 6

Red Peppers Catalan-style

3 eggs
3 red peppers
18 canned anchovies
¾ cup black olives
sprig parsley
3 slightly underripe tomatoes
2 cloves garlic
¼ cup olive oil
1 tablespoon wine vinegar
salt and pepper

1 Put the eggs into a saucepan of cold salted water. Boil them for 10 minutes over low heat, then cool in cold water. Shell and quarter them.

2 Broil the red peppers under high heat or hold them in a flame on a fork until the skin bubbles and darkens. Then hold them under cold water and peel. Split them in two, discarding the seeds and cut the flesh in thin strips.

3 Wash the anchovies under the cold tap to lose some of the salt and separate the fillets. Dry them.

4 Pit the olives. Wash, dry and chop the parsley. Wash, dry and quarter the tomatoes.

5 Peel the garlic and crush it with a spoonful of oil. Use this to season the anchovy fillets.

6 Arrange the peppers in the center of a round dish. Sprinkle the rest of the oil and the vinegar over them. Season with salt and pepper. Arrange the quartered tomatoes and hard-boiled eggs around the edge.

7 Use the anchovy fillets and the black olives to garnish the dish. Sprinkle with the chopped parsley and serve cold.

Serves 6

Taramasalata

6¾ **cups stale white breadcrumbs**
½ **cup milk**
2½ **lemons**
½ **cup cod roe**
⅔ **cup olive oil**
6 **tablespoons heavy cream**
¼ **cup black olives**
pinch paprika

1 Put the breadcrumbs into a bowl. Add the milk and mix well. Put it into a conical strainer and squeeze well to remove as much moisture as possible.

2 Cut and squeeze 1 lemon. Remove the skin from the cod roe.

3 Mix the breadcrumbs and the cod roe in the bowl. Add the olive oil and lemon juice little by little, mixing with a wooden spoon. Then blend in as much of the cream as is needed to give the taramasalata the consistency of a firm mayonnaise.

4 Wash and dry the other lemons. Cut them into quarters.

5 Put the taramasalata pâté into a dish. Surround with black olives and the lemon quarters and sprinkle with paprika. Serve very cold with hot toast or with French bread.

Serves 6

Taramasalata — this fish roe pâté is one of the most popular Greek appetizers

Lobster with Avocados

2 lbs. live lobster
sea salt
1 bouquet garni
1 small cucumber
2 avocados
2 tablespoons gin
½ teaspoon Tabasco sauce
salt and pepper
1¼ cups mayonnaise
pinch cayenne pepper
½ teaspoon paprika

1 Wash the lobster.

2 Boil water in a large saucepan with a handful of sea salt and the bouquet garni. Drop the lobster into the boiling water and cook for about 10 minutes.

3 Drain the lobster and let cool.

4 Peel the cucumber and split in two lengthwise. Take out the seeds with a small spoon. Grate the flesh of the cucumber, put it into a bowl and let drain without salting it.

5 Cut the avocados into halves, remove the pits, and, with a melon baller, scoop the flesh into balls.

6 When the lobster are cold, remove the meat from the tails.

7 Put the avocado balls and the lobster tails into a glass serving bowl. Pour over the gin and Tabasco sauce. Season with a little salt and pepper and mix well. Leave to marinate for about 20 minutes.

8 Lay a piece of cheesecloth over a colander. Pour in the cucumber pulp, and press down well to extract as much water as possible. Blend this pulp into the mayonnaise, folding it in gently. Then season with cayenne.

9 Pour the cucumber mayonnaise over the lobster and avocado, mixing well. Sprinkle with paprika and serve very cold.

Serves 4

Crab and Avocado Cocktail

4 eggs
½ lb. crabmeat
1 tablespoon tomato paste
1¼ cups mayonnaise
salt and pepper
3 avocados
paprika

1 Put 6 small glass dishes into the refrigerator.

2 Cook the eggs in boiling water for 10 minutes. Cool them in cold water and then shell them.

3 Flake the crabmeat, removing the cartilage. Add the tomato paste to the mayonnaise. Pass the hard-boiled eggs through a food mill or chop them.

4 Mix together the crabmeat, chopped eggs and the mayonnaise in a bowl. Season.

5 Cut the avocados in half, take out the pits, cut the flesh into large cubes and place them in the chilled dishes. Cover with the crab mixture and sprinkle with paprika. Chill until ready to serve.

Serves 6

Peaches Filled with Crab — a mixture of fruit and fish makes an interesting light first course

Tomatoes Stuffed with Anchovies and Rice

6 firm tomatoes
salt
¾ cup long grain rice
24 canned anchovy fillets
24 black olives
1 small bulb fennel
2 shallots
chopped parsley
1 green pepper
juice of ½ lemon
1¼ cups mayonnaise

1 Scoop out the tomatoes. Wash the rice under running cold water until the water is clear.

2 Bring to a boil a pan of salted water, twice the volume of the rice (i.e. 1½ cups). Add the rice, simmer for about 12 minutes or until tender, then drain and leave until cold.

3 Put aside 6 anchovy fillets and 6 olives. Chop the rest of the anchovies. Pit the olives and cut into quarters.

4 Trim the fennel, wash, dry and chop. Peel and chop the shallots. Wash, dry and chop the parsley.

Wash and dry the pepper; cut it in half, remove the seeds and white membrane and chop finely.

5 Add the lemon juice to the mayonnaise. Add the cooked rice, chopped anchovies, olives, shallots, fennel, pepper and the parsley to the mayonnaise. Fold carefully together.

6 Rinse and dry the tomatoes. Fill with the rice salad and make a dome on top. Top with an olive and a rolled anchovy fillet. Arrange the stuffed tomatoes on a serving dish and refrigerate for 1 hour before serving.

Serves 6

Peaches Filled with Crab

5 large peaches
¼ lb. crabmeat
½ cup heavy cream
¼ teaspoon lemon juice
2 teaspoons brandy
8 lettuce leaves
large pinch paprika
salt and pepper

1 Peel the peaches: halve them and remove the pits.

2 Drain the crab, and mash the crabmeat together with 1 of the peaches in a basin.

3 Add the cream, lemon juice, brandy, paprika, salt and pepper, and blend all the ingredients together well.

4 Wash the lettuce leaves, and dry them on absorbent paper. Make a bed of the leaves on a flat serving dish, and place a peach half on each of the leaves. Fill each peach half with the crab mixture.

5 Chill the dish for at least 1 hour before serving.

Serves 4

Tomatoes Stuffed with Anchovies and Rice — this simple dish is good for buffet parties

Pâtés and Terrines

Pâtés and terrines are well-seasoned savory meat, game or fish mixtures. They are generally cooked in casseroles or earthenware terrines — hence the name — in the oven and then served cold. Smooth or coarse, these preparations always include a proportion of fat and some alcohol — usually sherry or brandy — which enhances the flavor and storing quality of the pâté or terrine.

Sometimes slices of fatty bacon are used to line the dish so the fat mixture helps to lubricate the meat and keep it moist.

Liver Pâté

3 tablespoons butter
¼ cup flour
2¼ cups milk
salt
pinch cayenne pepper
pinch ground nutmeg
1 lb. chicken livers
2 cloves garlic
small bunch parsley
¼ cup brandy
¾ cup heavy cream
5 eggs plus 5 egg yolks

1 Melt 3 tablespoons butter in small pan. Blend in the flour with a wooden spoon and cook for a few minutes, but without letting it brown.

2 Little by little, add the milk, still beating well. Bring it to a boil, add salt, a pinch of cayenne pepper and a pinch of nutmeg. Let the mixture cook for 5 minutes.

3 Pass this white sauce through a fine strainer, and then let it cool.

4 Grind the livers. Peel and chop the garlic. Wash and dry the parsley, then chop it to produce 1 tablespoon. Add these ingredients to the liver.

5 Add the cold sauce. Mix it in, then beat in the brandy and the cream.

6 Preheat the oven to 350°F.

7 Add 5 whole eggs to the meat, then the egg yolks. Taste and adjust the seasoning.

8 Butter a 6¼-cup soufflé dish. Pour the liver mixture into it. Put the mold into a roasting pan half-filled with hot water.

9 Put the pan and soufflé mold into the oven to cook for 40 minutes.

10 Warm a serving plate.

11 When it is cooked, cool, then turn out the pâté and put it on the warm serving plate. Serve it right away, cut into slices like a cake, coated with a tomato or Nantua (shrimp) sauce.

Serves 4–6

Rabbit and Pork Terrine

1 onion
1 clove garlic
2 cloves
1 rabbit, cleaned and skinned, and with its liver
salt and pepper
3 cups dry white wine
1 bouquet garni

For the forcemeat:
liver of the rabbit
¼ lb. meat from a ham shank
¼ lb. lean pork
¼ lb. fat bacon
1 egg
¼ cup brandy
grated nutmeg
3 tablespoons butter
1 knuckle of veal
½ calf's foot

(left) Terrine of Turkey or Game ▶ (right) Chicken Pâté — can be served with toast or sliced with salad garnish

1 Peel the onion and slice into rounds. Peel the clove of garlic and stick it with the cloves.

2 Place the rabbit in a dish. Season with salt and pepper and pour over the white wine. Add the onion, garlic stuck with cloves and the bouquet garni and marinate for 24 hours in the refrigerator.

3 Next day make the forcemeat. Wash and finely chop the rabbit liver, the ham, pork, bacon and mix well together. Break the egg and stir into the meat mixture, together with the brandy, salt and pepper to taste and a little grated nutmeg. Blend well.

4 Strain off the marinade from the rabbit, reserving the liquid, and cut the rabbit in half across below the chest opening it up, cutting away and discarding the ribs. Stuff the rabbit with the forcemeat. Pull the stomach skin to enclose the stuffing and tie securely or sew up with a trussing needle and string.

5 Heat the butter in a deep heavy-based pan and brown the rabbit on all sides. Add the knuckle of veal and the ½ calf's foot and brown. Remove the pan from the heat, pour on the reserved marinade, bring to a boil, cover with a lid and cook slowly for about 2 hours. Take the veal out of the pan. Remove the bones and cut the meat into slices. Remove the string from the rabbit, take out the bones and cut the meat into strips. Arrange the meat slices and forcemeat in a large terrine or loaf pan.

6 Strain the cooking liquid through a strainer and pour over the meat to cover. Cool and then put the terrine in the refrigerator overnight so the liquid gels; serve the terrine cold with toast or French bread.

Serves 8

Terrine of Turkey

½ cup butter
3 cups cooked turkey
½ lb. sliced boiled ham
2 cloves garlic
1 lb. sausage meat
2 eggs
1 teaspoon finely chopped
   tarragon
1 tablespoon finely chopped
   parsley
¼ cup brandy
½ teaspoon salt
freshly ground black pepper
½ lb. bacon, thinly sliced

1 Remove the butter from the refrigerator to soften.

2 Cut the turkey into small pieces and put aside. Dice the ham.

3 Peel and crush the garlic and mix with the sausage meat, ham, eggs, tarragon, parsley, brandy, salt, pepper and butter in a large bowl.

4 Line a 3-pint casserole with three-quarters of the bacon. Top with a layer of sausage mixture and then a layer of turkey or game bird pieces. Repeat until all the ingredients are used. Top with a layer of sausage meat, then with the remaining bacon. Cover the casserole.

5 Preheat the oven to 375°F.

6 Place the casserole in a pan filled with enough hot water to come two-thirds of the way up and bake in the oven for 2 hours.

7 Cool and chill the terrine, with a weight on top, for at least 4 hours before serving with freshly made toast.

Serves 8

Chicken Pâté

½ cup butter
4 cups cooked chicken or turkey
   meat
½ lb. cooked pork
½ lb. cooked ham
2 cloves garlic
3 scallions
1 medium onion
1 tablespoon finely chopped
   parsley
1 bay leaf
¼ teaspoon thyme
½ teaspoon salt
freshly ground black pepper
2 eggs

1 tablespoon flour
¼ cup brandy
½ lb. bacon

1 Take the butter out of the refrigerator to soften.

2 Grind the chicken, pork and ham or chop them into very small pieces. Peel and crush the garlic and finely chop all the onions. Add the garlic, onion, parsley, bay leaf and thyme to the meat. Season with salt and pepper.

3 Lightly beat the eggs and add them to the meat mixture with the flour, butter and brandy. Stir until well combined.

4 Line a 3-pint casserole with the bacon slices. Add the meat mixture and top with the remaining bacon. Cover the casserole.

5 Preheat the oven to 350°F.

6 Place the casserole in a pan filled with enough hot water to come two-thirds of the way up, and cook in the oven for 1 hour.

7 Remove the pâté from the oven, cool and place a weight on top.

8 Refrigerate for at least 1 day before slicing and serving.

Serves 10

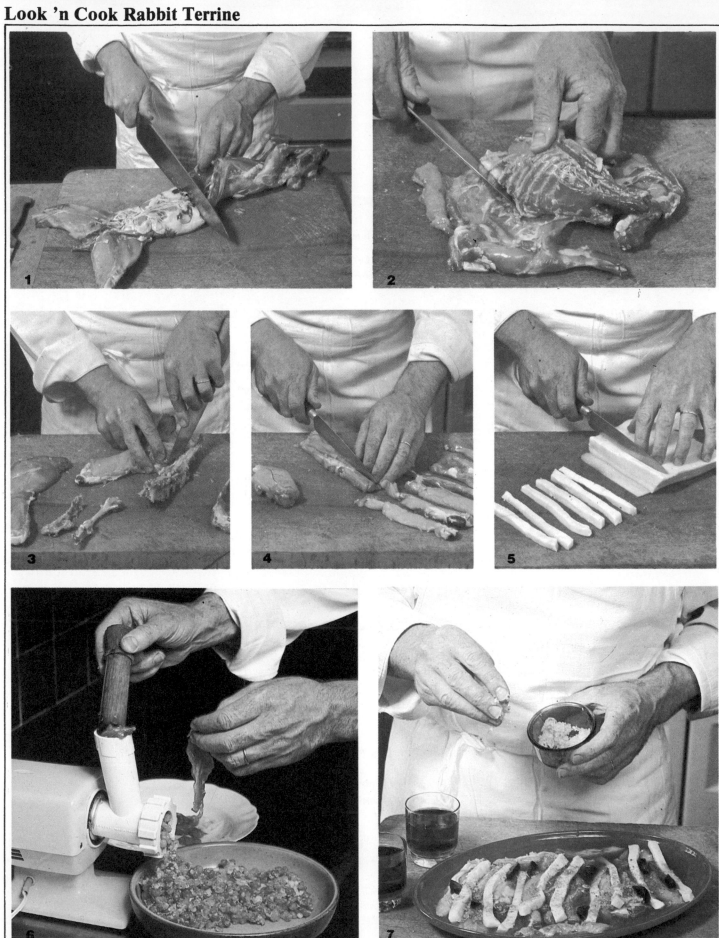

1 and 2 Bone the rabbit completely 3 and 4 Slice the meat from the hind end and the legs 5 Cut the salt pork into strips 6 Add the diced rabbit and pork and the strips of salt pork to the rest of the ingredients for the stuffing and leave to soak 7 and 8 Remove the strips of meat. Grind the rest of the mixture and weigh 9 Mix the ground meat, eggs, salt, cream, marinade liquid and garlic together 10 Line the dish with salt pork 11 Fill the dish with layers of stuffing and rabbit and salt pork slices. Finish with a layer of stuffing 12 Cover with the lining fat and garnish with rosemary and a halved bay leaf. Cover and cook in a pan of water 13 Cool the pâté under pressure 14 If liked, spoon aspic jelly over the top

Rabbit Terrine

1 large rabbit, skinned and cleaned
1 onion
½ lb. salt pork
9 ozs. lean pork
pinch allspice
1 teaspoon crushed thyme
1 teaspoon crushed bay leaf
pepper
1 bunch parsley
2 tablespoons olive oil
½ cup brandy
6 ozs. finely sliced salt pork
salt
1 egg
2 tablespoons heavy cream
1 clove garlic

1 Bone the rabbit entirely (you can have it done by your butcher). Cut the flesh of the saddle and legs into long slices ½ inch thick. Put them into a bowl. Peel the onion and cut into thin slices. Dice the rest of the rabbit flesh and the lean pork and the salt pork into strips. Put everything into the bowl with the allspice, thyme, bay leaves, pepper, parsley, oil and brandy. Mix. Cover the bowl and leave to marinate for 12 hours in a cool place.

2 Put the fine slices of salt pork to soak for at least 30 minutes in a large bowl of water. Change the water 2 or 3 times.

3 Drain the rabbit and pork mixture and keep the marinade. Put the long thin slices of flesh aside. Put the rest of the ingredients through the grinder or chop them. Weigh the mixture obtained. Measure 2 teaspoons of salt for each 1 lb. of mixture.

4 Put the mixture in a bowl with the salt, the egg, the cream and the marinade liquid. Peel and crush the garlic. Add it to the stuffing. Mix with a wooden spoon until smooth.

5 Drain the fine slices of salt pork and dry it on absorbent paper. Spread it and line the sides and base of a terrine. Cover the bottom with a layer of stuffing. Over it place a few long slices of rabbit. Put another layer of stuffing and so on until all the ingredients have been used, finishing with a layer of stuffing. Cover with another round of salt pork to enclose it. Preheat the oven to 400°F.

6 Cover the terrine. Put it in a shallow dish full of water. Cook in the oven for approximately 1 hour 30 minutes.

7 When the pâté is cooked, uncover it. Over it place a small board with a weight on top and let it cool. Keep it in the refrigerator until served.

Serves 12

Tip: To find out if the pate is cooked, make sure that the fat that comes up to the surface is quite clear.

Veal and Orange Pâté

3 lbs. fillet of veal
salt and pepper
pinch ground ginger
cayenne pepper
4 oranges
¼ cup brandy
½ cup medium dry white wine
1 envelope unflavored gelatin
¾ lb. bacon
1 firm ripe tomato
1 bunch watercress

1 Cut the veal into large pieces about 1½ inches square and put into a mixing bowl. Season with salt and pepper, ginger and a generous pinch of cayenne pepper.

2 Cut 2 oranges into halves and squeeze the juice into a bowl. Add the brandy and white wine; mix together well and pour over veal. Allow to stand for about 2½ hours.

3 To prepare gelatin, place 2½ cups water in a pan, sprinkle gelatin over water and stir well. Let stand for 5 minutes. Gently heat mixture until dissolved.

4 Pour a little gelatin into an ovenproof dish and let set. Remove peel from remaining two oranges and use strips of peel to make leaf shapes (see illustration). Place orange leaves on aspic in dish. Segment one orange and arrange segments in middle of dish to form a star. Slice remaining orange and reserve. Pour a little more gelatin over orange and let set. Set rest of gelatin in a roasting tin for use as a garnish.

5 Cut bacon into matchstick strips. Carefully arrange orange slices around side of dish. Place a layer of marinated veal in dish and cover with half the bacon strips. Repeat layering, finishing with the veal mixture. Pour the marinating liquor over meat.

6 Preheat oven to 425°F. Cover pâté and cook for 1¼ hours. Remove dish from oven and cover with a plate or pan lid. Place heavy weight on top and leave overnight.

7 When cool, turn pâté onto a serving dish. Chop gelatin in tin coarsely and arrange around dish.

8 Peel tomato, remove top and scoop out seeds. Cut a thin strip of tomato and roll up to form a flower shape. Decorate top of pâté with a few watercress leaves and tomato flower. Garnish dish with watercress.

Serves 8

Rabbit and Pork Terrine — a substantial enough dish to be served alone or with French bread for a light lunch

Prepare the fish and make the panada (see page 80).
1 Cook the panada until smooth and thick **2** Sauté the mushrooms, add the shallots and sauté until soft.

Remove **3** Add the cubed fish, cook until golden, then remove **4** Pour in the wine and boil, stirring in all the sediment **5** and **6** Put back the fish, mushrooms and

shallots and stir in the parsley **7** and **8** Blend the fish fillets with 2 egg whites **9** Add the panada, blend and turn into a bowl **10** Stir in the whipped cream **11** and

12 Fold in the fish and mushroom mixture, spoon into a greased terrine and cook

Fish Terrine

⅓ cup butter
3 lbs. firm white fish (e.g. pike, haddock, cod)
3 eggs
1 cup flour
salt and pepper
¾ cup milk
3½ cups button mushrooms
2 shallots
½ cup dry white wine
½ tablespoon chopped parsley
1 pint heavy cream

1 Take the butter out of the refrigerator to soften.

2 Fillet and skin the fish. Put in a basin, cover, and put in the refrigerator.

3 Work 3 tablespoons of the butter in a bowl to soften. Separate the eggs, and beat in the egg yolks and flour to make a stiff paste (panada); add salt and pepper.

4 Bring the milk to a boil in a saucepan, pour onto the panada, little by little, whisking all the time, then turn the mixture into a heavy pan. Cook over low heat, stirring with a wooden spoon all the time, until the mixture comes away cleanly from the sides of the pan. Lightly grease a plate, put the panada on it, cool, then chill in the refrigerator.

5 Peel and wipe the mushrooms. Slice them and sauté in 1½ tablespoons butter. Peel and finely chop the shallots; and add them to the saute pan. Cook very gently for about 3 minutes; season with salt and pepper, then turn the mixture into a bowl.

6 Put the sauté pan back on moderate heat; put in the fish and cook till golden-brown, then turn the fish into the bowl. Place the sauté pan on high heat, add the wine and boil for 2 minutes, stirring and scraping across the bottom of the pan to incorporate all the drippings. Reduce to half the quantity, then return the contents of the bowl to the sauté pan. Sprinkle with chopped parsley, add salt and pepper; blend together well and spoon back into the bowl.

7 Season the fish fillets with salt and pepper. Put them in a blender with 2 egg whites and the panada; blend until smooth.

8 Whip the cream until stiff, then stir into the fish mixture and blend again. Turn the mixture into a casserole or bowl. Stir in the mushrooms, shallots and fish.

9 Preheat the oven to 325°F. Lightly butter the terrine with 1½ tablespoons butter; spoon in the mixture and press down well. Cover and seal the terrine, then cook in a pan of water in the oven for about 1½ hours.

10 Cool, then chill until ready to serve.

Serves 10–12

Fish terrine — slicing the terrine into individual portions for serving

A large number of herbs — both fresh and dried — can be used to give extra flavor and interest to a wide variety of dishes. Try experimenting with their very individual flavors and using them as garnishes on all kinds of soups, sauces, vegetables and meat dishes.

Sautéed Chicken with Chervil

3 lbs. chicken
2 tablespoons flour
salt and pepper
2 tablespoons olive oil
2 tablespoons butter
4 cups mushrooms
3 shallots
½ cup brandy (optional)
½ cup dry white wine
1 cup fresh tomato sauce, or ½ cup tomato paste plus ½ cup stock
1 bouquet garni
small sprig chervil
1 teaspoon cornstarch

1 Cut up the chicken.

2 Put the flour onto a plate. Season the chicken pieces with salt and pepper and roll them in the flour.

3 Heat the oil and the butter together in a deep pan and when it is hot, brown the pieces of chicken on both sides (about 15 minutes).

4 Meanwhile, wipe, trim and slice the mushrooms. Peel the shallots and chop them.

5 Add the mushrooms and shallots to the pan and brown them. Then pour in the brandy, if used, and ignite it.

6 Add the white wine, the stock and the tomato sauce, or paste and stock if used, to the pan. Add the bouquet garni. Cover and simmer the mixture for 30 minutes over low heat.

7 Warm a serving dish. Wash and chop the chervil.

8 When the chicken is cooked, remove the pieces from the pan. Blend the cornstarch with a little of the hot sauce. Pour it back into the pan and mix in with a wooden spoon. Let it cook for 3 minutes, then coat the chicken with the sauce and the mushrooms. Sprinkle on the chervil and serve hot, with boiled rice served separately.

Serves 4

❧

Tarragon Chicken Croquettes

2 whole chicken breasts, boned, cut in half
¼ lb. very cold butter
4 ice cubes
2 eggs
salt and white pepper
1 teaspoon dried tarragon
oil for deep frying
1½ cups dried white breadcrumbs

1 Place a chicken breast between 2 sheets of wetted wax paper and beat with a cutlet mallet to flatten. Repeat the flattening process with the remaining chicken breasts.

2 Cut the butter into 4 equal flat pieces. Put an ice cube in the center of each one and put a piece of butter onto each piece of meat. Roll and tie, making sure the butter is completely enclosed, and place in the refrigerator for 30 minutes.

3 Beat the eggs, salt and pepper and the tarragon vigorously in a bowl.

4 Heat the oil in the deep fat fryer to 375°F.

5 Take the chicken croquettes out of the refrigerator and untie them. Dip them in the beaten egg mixture, then roll in the breadcrumbs.

6 Press the breadcrumbs firmly onto the chicken with a flat-bladed knife.

7 When the hot oil is at the correct frying temperature ease the croquettes into the fat and fry for about 7 minutes until golden-brown.

8 Drain them on absorbent paper and serve very hot on a bed of lettuce, accompanied by peas and sautéed potatoes.

Serves 4

Tip: You can substitute turkey cutlets for the chicken breasts.

❧

Tomatoes with Cream

6 medium, round and not-too-ripe tomatoes
6 small shallots
sprig chervil
½ cup sour cream
freshly ground white pepper
salt

1 Wash and dry the tomatoes. Slice off a cap from the end opposite the stalk end of each. Scoop out the pulp with a small spoon or melon baller, removing the core and seeds. Lightly salt the inside to draw out excess moisture, and turn the tomatoes upside-down on a dish to drain.

2 Peel and chop the shallots finely. Wash, dry and chop the chervil, putting aside 1 tablespoon for the decoration. Put the cream, the rest of the chopped chervil and the shallots into a bowl. Add a little salt, and lots of pepper and mix well with a fork.

3 Arrange the tomato shells on a serving dish, fill with the seasoned cream mixture. Sprinkle the tops with chopped chervil. Place the dish in the refrigerator for an hour before serving very cold.

Serves 6

Variations: Substitute the shallots and chervil with garlic, chopped parsley or chives. You can improve the seasoning of the cream with the strained juice of half a lemon.

A vital ingredient in French cooking, virtually replacing parsley, chervil is a pale green aromatic herb.

All about herbs and their uses

Mint *This is a popular herb which is used as a flavoring for boiled new potatoes and peas and as a garnish for fruit and iced drinks. It is probably best known for its use in mint sauce or jelly to accompany roast lamb.*

Sorrel *The leaves of this herb have a pungent acid flavor and the young ones are used in salads. The older plant can be cooked in the same way as spinach and is used to flavor sauces and soups. Sorrel is also known as dock.*

Thyme *The excellent flavor of thyme means that it is used extensively in the kitchen and is one of the basic ingredients of a bouquet garni. The leaves contain an oil called thymol which aids the digestion of fatty foods. Thyme can be used with cheese dishes, shellfish and poultry stuffing and as a garnish for vegetables.*

Rosemary *The leaves are used both fresh and dried and go well with beef, salmon, duck, boiled ham and pork. Rosemary can also be used with sweet dishes such as jellos, fruit salads and biscuits.*

Marjoram *There are three types of marjoram, sweet marjoram being the one most often used for flavoring. It can be added to soups, stews, cheese and egg dishes, and salads and blends well with other herbs such as thyme.*

Fennel *This herb is related to dill but is sweeter and more aromatic. The digestive properties of fennel make it a good accompaniment to oily fish dishes, and it is also used to flavor soups, sauces, salads, cakes and pastry.*

Sage *This is a slightly bitter herb which, because of its strong flavor, should be used carefully. Sage is probably best known for its use with onion in poultry stuffings, but it also gives a good flavor to peas and beans. Chopped fresh leaves can be added to salads, pickles and cheese, and the dried leaves to casseroles and sausage meat.*

Bay Leaves *These have a strong spicy flavor which goes well with game, meat, fish, poultry, salads, sauces and vegetables. Bay leaves are a basic ingredient of a bouquet garni and can be added to the milk used for custards, molds, and milk puddings and to the stock for boiling fish. Their flavor becomes stronger if they are crushed or dried.*

Chives *Chive is a member of the leek and onion family and, as would be expected, the flavor is reminiscent of onion. The thin, tubular stalks are a bright green color and so look very attractive chopped into short lengths and sprinkled over soups or mixed into pale dishes such as potato salad and cream cheese.*

Dill *Dill leaves are blue-green and feathery in appearance and their flavor is similar to aniseed and caraway. They can be chopped and added to salads, green vegetables, soups and stews, but because their flavor soon disappears when they are cooked, they should be added to hot dishes just before serving. Dill adds flavor to pickles and is particularly suited to use with fish dishes.*

Basil *The large, heart-shaped leaves of basil have a peppery flavor and can be used in combination with other herbs such as rosemary, sage and oregano. The flavor develops with cooking so basil should be used carefully. This herb is particularly effective with vegetables which have little flavor and with chicken, egg and rice dishes.*

Mint

Sorrel

Thyme

Rosemary

Marjoram

Fennel

Lemon sage

Bay leaves

Chives

Sage

Dill

Basil

Stuffed Small Tomatoes

24 small tomatoes
6 ozs. cream cheese
1 cup cottage cheese
½ teaspoon mixed herbs
24 stuffed olives

1 Wash and dry the tomatoes. Cut a slice from the base of the tomatoes opposite the stalk end and carefully hollow out the tomatoes with a little spoon.

2 Mix the cheeses and mixed herbs together and fill the tomatoes with them.

3 Decorate each with an olive and chill in the refrigerator until served.

Serves 24

Red Currant Charlotte with Mint

4 cups red currants, fresh or
   frozen
2 tablespoons mint
1 tablespoon water
¼ cup sugar

For the Charlotte Topping:
2 cups fresh white breadcrumbs
3 ozs. shredded beef suet
⅓ cup light brown sugar
½ teaspoon ground cinnamon
2 tablespoons butter

1 If using fresh fruit, wash it and then top and tail it using kitchen scissors. Wash and finely chop the mint.

2 Place the red currants in a pan, together with the mint, water and sugar. Bring to a boil, then reduce the heat and simmer for 5 minutes.

3 Preheat the oven to 375°F. Lightly grease an 8-inch soufflé dish.

4 Mix together the breadcrumbs, suet, brown sugar and cinnamon.

5 Pour half the fruit mixture into the bottom of the dish. Spoon on half the Charlotte mixture. Pour the remaining fruit on top, topping it with the breadcrumb mixture. Dot the surface with little pats of butter and bake in the oven for about 45 minutes.

6 Serve hot, with fresh cream or custard.

Serves 4

Haddock Mousse with Herbs

1 onion
3 canned anchovies
½ lemon
1 tablespoon lemon balm leaves
1 cup water
1 small bay leaf
1 lb. smoked haddock
salt and pepper
1¼ cups made up unflavored gelatin
   using packet and poaching liquid
2 eggs
1 tablespoon dry sherry
½ cup heavy cream
1 small cucumber
small bunch watercress

1 Peel and slice the onion; drain and chop the anchovies; remove the zest from the lemon, using a grater, and squeeze out the juice; wash and finely chop the lemon balm leaves.

2 Place the water, onion, bay leaf and smoked haddock in a pan; add salt and pepper. Bring it to a boil, reduce the heat and poach the fish gently for about 10 minutes.

3 Remove the fish, setting the cooking liquid aside. Flake the fish into a bowl, removing any skin and bones.

4 Strain the cooking liquid, make up gelatin by following the instructions on the packet and using the reserved cooking liquid; make up the volume with water. Let cool.

5 Separate the eggs, and beat the yolks, lemon zest and juice, sherry, anchovies and balm together in a bowl. Beat in the cooled gelatin when it is nearly set but still just liquid, then gently stir in the fish. Leave this mixture aside until it begins to set.

6 When setting starts, beat the egg whites until they stand in stiff peaks, then stiffly whip the cream. Fold the cream in fish mixture first, using a metal spoon, and then the egg whites.

7 Spoon the mixture into a lightly oiled mold (6¼-cup capacity) and refrigerate until the mousse is completely set.

8 Turn the mousse onto an oval plate and decorate with cucumber butterflies and small sprigs of watercress. Serve cold.

Serves 4

Peperonata

1 lb. red and green peppers
½ wine glass olive oil
2 cloves garlic
3 large onions
2 bay leaves
4 small tomatoes
salt and pepper
1 tablespoon white vinegar

1 Hold the peppers over a flame until the skin blackens and wrinkles, then peel it off. Cut the peppers in two, remove the seeds and white fiber and slice peppers thinly and evenly. Wipe the slices.

2 Heat the oil in a large pan on gentle heat.

3 Meanwhile, peel and chop the garlic and onions. Put them into the hot oil and brown, stirring with a wooden spoon, over low heat. Then add the bay leaves and sliced peppers. Cook slowly, stirring from time to time, for 15 minutes.

4 Meanwhile, boil water in a pot.

5 Immerse the tomatoes for 30 seconds in this boiling water, then drain, put into cold water and then peel them. Cut them in quarters and remove the seeds.

6 Add the tomatoes to the peppers, with salt and pepper. Stir, then cover and leave to stew slowly for 30 minutes.

7 Three or four minutes before the cooking is completed, add the vinegar to the vegetable mixture. Increase the heat, and cook until the liquid reduces and thickens, stirring all the time so that the peperonata does not stick to the bottom of the pan.

8 Pour the mixture into a salad bowl and leave to cool completely before serving.

Hard-boiled Egg, Anchovy and Tomato Canapés

6 eggs
12 slices tomato
¼ cup butter
6 square slices sandwich loaf
36 anchovy fillets in oil
few sprigs fennel

1 Boil the eggs for 10 minutes, then cool in cold water. Peel them.

2 Cut each slice of tomato in three curved strokes in order to obtain 3 crescents. Put all 36 crescents to one side.

3 Butter the slices of bread and cut them into halves diagonally.

4 Cut each egg into 6 slices. Decorate each canapé with 3 slices of egg. Then place a rolled anchovy and an arc of tomato onto each slice of egg. Decorate.

Serves 4

Ham and Fruit Hors d'Oeuvre

½ lb. cooked ham
2 grapefruit
1 large orange
2 apples
2 lemons
1 small head lettuce
bunch chervil
1 cucumber
1¼ cups mayonnaise
paprika
salt and pepper

1 Cut the ham into very thin strips.

2 Halve the grapefruits and scoop out the flesh with a grapefruit knife.

3 Peel the orange and separate the sections. Peel the apples, cut them in quarters, removing the core and seeds. Slice the quarters thinly.

4 Cut and squeeze 1 lemon, reserving the juice. Wash and dry the second and cut it in quarters.

5 Clean the lettuce, taking off the large leaves, and leaving the heart intact. Wash and dry the salad and the chervil.

6 Peel the cucumber, split it in two and remove the seeds. Cut the 2 halves in thin slices. Sprinkle with salt and leave to draw out the excess moisture while continuing with other preparations.

7 Put into a bowl the grapefruit pieces, orange sections and sliced apples.

8 Drain and dry the cucumber and add it to the other ingredients. Pour on half the lemon juice, sprinkle with paprika and mix gently. Stir the remaining lemon juice into the mayonnaise.

9 Arrange the large lettuce leaves around the edge of a small salad bowl. Put the fruit mixture in the center, coat with mayonnaise, and arrange the ham strips on the top.

10 Put the lettuce heart in the middle of the dish and garnish with lemon quarters. Scatter chopped chervil over the top and serve cold.

Serves 6

Bacon Rigodon Flan

1¾ cups milk
½ lb. thin smoked lean bacon
5 tablespoons butter
3 tablespoons potato flour or cornstarch
6 eggs
scant 1 cup cream
pinch ground mixed spice (see page 86)
pinch thyme
salt and pepper

1 Bring the milk to a boil in a pan, then let it cool down. Slice the bacon.

2 Heat half of the butter in a skillet and put the slices in to fry.

3 Mix the potato flour to a smooth paste with some of the cooled milk. Break the eggs into a bowl, add the potato flour and beat it with a whisk while adding, little by little, the rest of the milk, the cream, the bacon, the ground mixed spice and the thyme. Add pepper and a very small amount of salt.

4 Preheat the oven to 375°F.

5 Butter an ovenproof pie pan with the rest of the butter, pour the mixture into it and cook it in the oven for 35 minutes. Serve lukewarm in the same dish.

Serves 6

Tip: If it turns too deep a color during the course of cooking, cover the pan with a sheet of foil.

Hot Appetizers

Shrimp Rissoles

1 medium onion
2 tablespoons olive oil
1½ cups shrimp, shelled and
   deveined
4 tablespoons finely chopped
   parsley
3 eggs, separated
2 tablespoons flour
1 teaspoon salt
freshly ground black pepper
shortcrust pastry made from 2
   cups flour
oil for deep frying

1 Finely chop the onion. Heat the oil in a skillet and fry the shrimp, onion and parsley over high heat for 4-5 minutes, stirring constantly.

2 Put the shrimp mixture into a large bowl and add the egg yolks, flour, salt and pepper. In another bowl beat the egg whites until they form stiff peaks; gently fold them into the shrimp mixture, using a metal spoon or spatula.

3 Roll out the pastry very thinly and cut into rounds with a 4-inch diameter pastry (cookie) cutter. Place a little of the shrimp mixture on half of each round. Moisten the edges of the pastry with cold water and fold over the filling. Pinch the edges together to seal.

4 Heat the oil in a deep fat fryer: it is ready when a little flour dropped in sizzles instantly. Put in the rissoles, a few at a time, and fry for about 4 minutes or until golden-brown.

5 Drain the rissoles on absorbent paper and serve hot.

Serves 4

Burgundy Snails

48 snails with the shells separate

For the Snail Paste:
1 cup butter
3 tablespoons parsley
1 tablespoon garlic
1½ tablespoons shallots
1 tablespoon salt
1 teaspoon freshly ground pepper

1 Cut the butter into small pieces and leave it to soften in a bowl. Wash and finely chop the parsley. Peel and chop the garlic and the shallots.

2 Mix together the softened butter, the salt, the pepper and the chopped garlic, shallots and parsley. Beat all the ingredients together with a wooden spoon. Put this butter into a piping (decorator's) bag fitted with a large plain pipe.

3 Pipe a little butter into each shell and then place a snail in each one as well. Finish by filling the shells completely with the flavored butter.

4 Preheat the oven to 350°F. Place the snails in their shells in a snail plate and then put the plate into the oven and serve the snails the moment that the butter begins to melt (about 7 minutes).

Serves 4

Tips:

1 If you do not want to use the snail shells, use instead the special snail plates available, with hollows for each snail.

Pipe or put a little snail butter in each hollow, then place a snail on top and then fill up with butter as before.

2 It is important to keep the snail shells firmly in place during heating, with their openings at the top so the butter does not run out when hot. A good way to keep the shells steady is to sit them on crumpled aluminum foil, lining each hollow.

Tomatoes with Beef Stuffing

4 large firm tomatoes
salt
½ lb. cold roast beef
2 onions
2 tablespoons butter
pepper
pinch mixed spice
1 tablespoon chopped parsley
2 tablespoons olive oil

1 Wash and dry the tomatoes. Cut out the places where the stalks were and cut a slice from the other end of each one.

2 Remove the seeds and cores with a small spoon but leave enough pulp for the tomatoes to stay firm. Sprinkle the insides with salt and leave upside down on a rack to drain.

3 Grind the beef and chop the onions. Melt the butter in a skillet and cook the onions over low heat for 6-7 minutes or until golden.

4 Add the ground beef to the onions. Turn up the heat and cook for 2-3 minutes, stirring well all the time. Add salt, pepper and the mixed spice.

5 Remove the stuffing from the heat and stir in the parsley.

6 Rinse and dry the tomatoes. Preheat the oven to 400°F.

7 Brush the bottom and sides of an ovenproof dish with the oil.

8 Stuff the tomatoes and put on their lids. Put them in the dish, cover with foil and bake for 20 minutes. Serve straight from the oven.

Serves 4

Tip: A good mixed spice mixture is: 1 tablespoon ground cloves, 2 tablespoons ground ginger, 3 tablespoons ground nutmeg.

Look 'n Cook Stuffed Tomatoes

1 Sauté the onions in the butter until golden, then add the beef and cook for a further 2-3 minutes. Mix in the spice and parsley 2 and 3 Stuff the tomatoes with the filling. Stand them in a greased ovenproof dish, replace the lids, and cover with foil 4 Cook for 20 minutes and serve from the dish

Baked Asparagus Italian-style

2 lbs. (28-30 spears) thin asparagus
salt
5 medium ripe tomatoes
pinch oregano
6 freshly milled peppercorns
1 clove garlic
6-oz. can tomato paste
small pinch sugar
3 tablespoons butter
2 tablespoons grated Parmesan cheese

1 Peel and wash the asparagus (see right) and trim off the tough ends. Tie in a bundle.

2 Heat 9 cups lightly salted water. As soon as it begins to boil, put in the tied asparagus and let boil for 15-20 minutes, depending on the quality of the asparagus (sample one to find out). Drain the asparagus and place on a folded cloth.

3 Plunge the tomatoes in boiling water. Skin them and cut into thin slices. Season with salt and oregano and the milled peppercorns. Let stand for 5 minutes.

4 In the meantime, peel the garlic and crush it completely. Empty the can of tomato paste into a bowl. Add the sugar and stir.

5 Preheat the oven to 375°F.

6 Melt the butter and put half in an oval ovenproof dish. Arrange the asparagus and the tomato paste in this dish in alternate layers, finishing with the tomato. Spread this evenly with the back of a knife blade. Arrange the sliced tomatoes on the top so that they cover the surface completely. Sprinkle with the rest of the melted butter and the Parmesan cheese.

7 Cook in the oven for 20 minutes.

8 Increase the heat of the oven to 425°F. and cook for another 10 minutes to brown the cheese.

Serves 4

Tip: The asparagus must be thoroughly peeled and trimmed. All the woody parts must be removed to make this dish work.

French Asparagus

2 lbs. (about 28 spears) asparagus
salt
2 tablespoons butter
¼ cup flour
1 tablespoon prepared French mustard
1 cup light cream
3 hard-boiled eggs
pepper
1 tablespoon chopped chervil and chives (mixed)

1 Tie prepared asparagus (see right) into 4 bundles and cook for 20 minutes or until tender in boiling salted water; lift out and keep warm. Reserve cooking liquid.

2 Melt the butter in a thick pan and then stir in the flour using a wooden spoon. Cook the mixture for a few minutes without allowing it to brown. Take the pan off the heat and beat in 1 cup asparagus water. Return the pan to the heat and cook for 6 minutes.

3 Add the mustard to the cream. Stir this mixture into the white sauce and cook very gently for 10 minutes. Cut 2 hard-boiled eggs into very small cubes and add to the sauce. Season with salt and pepper.

4 Finely chop the third egg and mix it with the chervil and chives. Put the well-drained bundles of asparagus onto a heated serving dish and sprinkle with the egg. Serve very hot with the sauce in a sauce boat.

Serves 4

Browned Asparagus

salt
2 lbs. (24-28 spears) asparagus
3 eggs
¾ cup light cream
1 cup grated Gruyère or Cheddar cheese
pepper
pinch grated nutmeg
2 tablespoons butter

1 Boil salted water in a large pot.

2 Peel and wash the asparagus (see right) and tie in bundles. Plunge them into the vigorously boiling water, cover, reduce the heat when the water boils again and leave to cook for about 20 minutes.

3 Meanwhile, put the eggs in a small saucepan. Cover with water, bring to a boil and cook for 12 minutes.

4 Place the eggs in cold water, then shell them and rub through a strainer into a bowl; add the cream and most of the grated cheese. Add salt, pepper and the grated nutmeg. Mix with a wooden spoon.

5 Heat the oven to 425°F.

6 Carefully drain the asparagus. Remove the string.

7 Butter an ovenproof dish. Put in a layer of asparagus. Cover with a layer of the cream, egg and cheese mixture. Continue in this way until all the ingredients are used up. Finish with a layer of the cream mixture.

8 Sprinkle on the remainder of the cheese, then flake the remaining butter on top. Put the dish into the oven and let brown for about 30 minutes. Serve in the same dish.

Serves 4

Tip: The asparagus spears must be well drained to prevent any water from diluting the sauce while in the oven.

1 Gently clean the point of each spear with a small knife 2 Lay the spears flat and peel away from the head with a potato peeler 3 Snap off the spear just above the coarse end 4 Wash the spears without soaking and tie them into bundles 5 Cut all the spears to the same length 6 The prepared asparagus

Spanish Artichokes

6 large artichokes
¾ cup long grain rice
2 peppers
1 onion
3 tomatoes
¾ lb. smoked lean bacon
2 cloves garlic
bunch parsley
5 tablespoons olive oil
pinch saffron
salt and pepper
½ lemon

1 Trim the artichokes by cutting the stalk and leaves 1¼ inches from the base. (Use a serrated knife or scissors for the leaves.) Wash and drain them.

2 Boil salted water in a large saucepan. Put in the artichokes and boil for 15 minutes.

3 Meanwhile, wash the rice until the water is quite clear.

4 Put the rice in twice its volume of boiling salted water, and simmer for 12 minutes.

5 Drain the rice, rinse it under cold running water, then drain once more.

6 Wash and dry the peppers. Split them in two and remove the seeds and white fiber. Dice. Peel and chop the onion. Peel the tomatoes, cut them in quarters, remove the seeds, then dice them also. Dice the bacon finely. Peel and chop the garlic cloves. Wash, dry and chop the parsley.

7 Heat 2 tablespoons olive oil in a sauté pan. Put in the diced bacon, onion and peppers, and fry.

8 When they are golden-brown, add the diced tomatoes, garlic, parlsey, saffron and rice. Season with salt and pepper. Stir for 3 or 4 minutes over moderate heat.

9 Drain the artichokes, and put them in cold water, then drain and dry. Pull the outside leaves apart and, with a small spoon, remove the hairy centers (chokes) and little leaves. Fill the artichokes with the rice mixture.

Trimmed and prepared artichoke in boiling water

10 Heat the rest of the oil in a sauté pan. Put in the artichokes, cover and leave to finish cooking on low heat for 40 minutes.

11 Squeeze the half lemon. Heat a serving dish.

12 Halfway through the cooking, add the lemon juice and 3 tablespoons hot water to the artichokes.

13 Arrange the artichokes on a serving dish and serve very hot.

Serves 6

Artichoke Hearts with Herbs

4 globe artichokes
½ lemon
large bunch chives, parsley and tarragon, mixed
3 tablespoons butter
salt and pepper

For the blanching mixture:
2½ lemons
6⅓ cups water
1 tablespoon flour

1 Prepare the artichokes to give you 4 hearts (see page 58), then rub each heart all over with a ½ lemon. Prepare the blanching mixture with the lemons, water and flour and cook the hearts in the boiling liquid for 40 minutes or until tender. Drain them, rinse under cold water and cool.

2 Wash the bunch of herbs, dry and chop finely.

3 Melt the butter in a skillet. Cut the hearts into pieces and sauté them until they are golden-brown, then add the chopped herbs. Add a little pepper, mixing with the wooden spoon.

4 Warm a vegetable dish. Put in the artichoke hearts and serve hot.

Serves 4

Artichokes Stuffed with Vegetables

8 medium globe artichokes
1 lemon
4 onions
4 carrots
¼ lb. lean bacon
scant 3 cups mushrooms
small bunch parsley
1 tablespoon olive oil
sprig sage
½ cup dry white wine
pinch dried thyme
salt and pepper

1 Break off the artichoke stems and rub each base with lemon. Also cut off the large leaves in a circle. Wash the artichokes under running water. Cook in boiling salted water for 25-30 minutes and then drain and keep hot.

2 Meanwhile, peel the onions and chop them roughly. Peel the carrots and cut them into matchsticks. Cut the bacon into small pieces. Prepare the mushrooms and cut into slices. Wash, dry and chop the parsley.

3 Fry the bacon and onions in the oil until the onions brown. Add the mushrooms, carrots, chopped pars-ley and sage. Let them brown also. Add the white wine and sprinkle in the thyme. Cover and simmer for about 20 minutes. Drain them and keep them hot.

4 Cut off the tops of the artichoke leaves and scoop out the choke. Stuff the artichokes with the bacon and vegetables.

Serves 8

Artichokes Stuffed with Vegetables — the shapely artichokes lend themselves to holding a variety of hot or cold fillings

Alsatian Gnocchi

10 medium potatoes
1 cup flour
2 eggs
pinch grated nutmeg
salt and pepper
2 tablespoons cream
½ cup grated cheese

1 Bring salted water to a boil in a pot. Wash 3 potatoes and cook them in the boiling water, unpeeled, for 20 minutes.

2 In the meantime, peel the rest of the potatoes. Grate them finely, then wrap in a clean dry cloth and twist the ends in opposite directions to squeeze out all the moisture.

3 Peel the cooked potatoes while still hot. Mash them with a fork and mix with the grated potatoes.

4 Add the flour, then the eggs, one by one, and the nutmeg. Season with salt and pepper. Blend thoroughly with a wooden spoon, to obtain a smooth mixture.

5 Bring lightly salted water in a large pot to boiling point.

6 Using two spoons, shape the mixture into small balls. Lower them gently into the boiling water and simmer for 7-8 minutes. Keep the heat low to prevent the gnocchi from disintegrating as they will do in rapidly boiling water.

7 In the meantime, heat the broiler.

8 Lift the gnocchi out of the water with a skimmer or a slotted spoon and drain them on a cloth.

9 Arrange the balls in a shallow flameproof dish and cover with the cream. Sprinkle with grated cheese. Place under the broiler until the cheese bubbles and begins to turn brown (about 10 minutes).

10 Remove from the broiler and serve at once in the dish in which it was cooked.

Serves 6

Gnocchi Paris-style

½ cup plus 1 tablespoon butter
1¼ cups water
salt and pepper
pinch grated nutmeg
scant 2 cups flour
4 eggs
1 cup grated Gruyère or Cheddar cheese
3 cups milk

1 To make the choux pastry, put ½ cup of butter into a saucepan with the water, a pinch of salt, a pinch of pepper and the nutmeg. Bring it to a boil over gentle heat.

2 When the liquid is boiling take the saucepan off the stove and put 1¾ cups of flour in all at once. Mix it in with a wooden spoon. Put the saucepan back on the stove and continue to stir the paste until it comes away from the sides and curls around the spoon.

3 Take the saucepan off the heat again and blend in the eggs one at a time, stirring vigorously all the time. Beat in half the grated cheese.

4 Heat salted water in a pot. When the water simmers, dampen a pastry bag, fitted with a medium plain pipe. Fill it with paste and pipe into the saucepan small pieces about ¾ inch long (see Tip). Leave them to poach, without boiling, for 6 minutes. Then cool the gnocchi in cold water.

5 Melt the rest of the butter in a saucepan. Add the rest of the flour. Stir it with a wooden spoon without allowing it to brown. Add the cold milk bit by bit, stirring all the time. Bring it to a boil. Add salt and pepper to taste, reduce the heat and cook for 6-8 minutes.

6 Preheat the oven to 400°F.

7 Pour a base of sauce into an oven-to-table gratin dish. Arrange the gnocchi on this sauce and cover with the rest of the white sauce. Sprinkle with the rest of the grated cheese and cook in the oven for about 20 minutes.

8 Serve the gnocchi immediately in the gratin dish.

Serves 4

Tip: Do not leave this dish to stand or the gnocchi will tend to collapse. To form the gnocchi: fill the pastry bag, place it on the edge of the saucepan and squeeze with the left hand. Allow about ¾ inch of pastry to come out and pinch it between the fingers of the right hand, or cut with a knife or scissors.

Fried Squid Savory

oil for deep frying
2 lbs. squid
½ cup beer
6 tablespoons flour
salt and pepper
bunch parsley

1 Heat the oil in a deep fat fryer to 350°F.

2 Clean the squid by cutting off the black pouch and the transparent cartilage. Cut off the transparent skin, wash in a lot of water and cut into long, fine strips. Lay them on absorbent paper.

3 Pour the beer into an earthenware pot. Put the flour in a separate bowl, add salt and pepper and mix. Tie a knot in each strip of squid and retain with a wooden cocktail stick.

4 Soak the knotted strips in beer, then toss them in flour, one at a time. Shake off excess flour, lower them into the hot oil and let them cook until brown.

5 Drain the squid. Arrange on a serving dish. Put the bunch of parsley into the hot oil and fry for 2 minutes.

6 Serve very hot with apéritifs.

Serves 4

Scallops with Sautéed Mushrooms

4½ cups mushrooms
1½ lemons
small bunch parsley
½ cup butter
24 scallops, fresh or frozen and
    thawed
1 clove garlic
3 shallots
1 tablespoon olive oil
salt and pepper

1 Wipe and trim the mushrooms and slice them finely. Squeeze the juice from the ½ lemon, and toss the mushrooms in it.

2 Wash and chop the parsley. Using a small vegetable knife score lines down the whole lemon, and then cut it into wedges.

3 Melt about 2 tablespoons of the butter in a small saucepan, add the mushrooms and let sauté gently for about 5 minutes, turning them frequently to prevent browning.

4 Wash the scallops in cold water, dry them and dice the white flesh. Peel and crush the garlic; peel and chop the shallots.

5 Put the oil and about 3 tablespoons of the butter into a skillet. When the butter is hot, add the chopped white meat, the shallots, half of the parsley and the garlic. Cook gently for about 10 minutes, stirring occasionally with a wooden spoon.

6 Wash scallop shells and spread the rest of the butter inside them.

7 Blend the mushrooms into the scallop mixture, and season well.

8 Spoon a little of the mixture into each of the scallop shells and garnish each with the remainder of the parsley and a wedge of lemon. Serve very hot.

Serves 6

Scallops and Mushrooms make a light, refreshing start to any meal

Fried Smelts

16 large fresh smelts
handful sea salt
1 tablespoon dry breadcrumbs
1 tablespoon light cream
1 egg
1 clove garlic
2 shallots
small bunch chives and chervil
salt and pepper
1¼ cups flour
oil for deep frying
1¼ cups milk
bunch parsley

1 Wash and dry the smelts. Place them in an earthenware dish. Sprinkle with the sea salt. Place in the refrigerator for 4 hours.

2 Mix the breadcrumbs and cream in a bowl. Crack an egg and separate the yolk from the white. Add the yolk to the bowl and mix again.

3 Peel the garlic and shallots. Chop them. Wash and dry the chives and chervil, chop them as well. Add these ingredients to the cream and breadcrumbs. Add salt and pepper. Mix thoroughly with a wooden spoon.

4 Pour the flour onto a plate. Heat the oil to 360°F.

5 Clean the smelts. Gut them, cut out the backbone and fill with the cream stuffing.

6 Put the stuffed smelts back into the earthenware dish, cover with the milk. Then dry them and dip into the flour one by one. Put them into a frying basket. Gently shake the basket to remove excess flour.

7 Lower the basket into the hot oil and leave to cook and brown.

8 Heat a serving dish. Wash the parsley, dry well.

9 When the fish have browned, drain them and arrange on the serving dish.

10 Lower the parsley into the oil.

Fry for 2 minutes, then drain it and arrange with the fish.

11 Serve very hot.

Serves 4

Tip: As it is necessary to open the smelts to remove the backbone, keep them closed with a wooden cocktail stick when stuffed.

Mushrooms Stuffed with Ham

16 large mushrooms
4½ cups small mushrooms
1½ lemons
4 shallots
5 tablespoons butter
3 tablespoons fresh breadcrumbs
2 tablespoons milk
1 bunch mixed herbs (parsley, chives)
¼ lb. cooked ham
1 tablespoon heavy cream
salt and pepper

1 Wash and dry the large and small mushrooms. Separate the stalks from the caps of the large mushrooms. Finely chop the stalks and the small mushrooms.

2 Squeeze the juice from the ½ lemon over the chopped mushrooms. Peel and chop the shallots.

3 Heat 2 tablespoons of the butter in a skillet. Sauté the shallots until soft. Stir in the chopped mushrooms and cook until all the liquid has evaporated.

4 Soak the breadcrumbs in a little milk, then squeeze to remove excess moisture. Wash and dry the herbs. Chop the ham and herbs together and mix them with the breadcrumbs. Add the cream and salt and pepper to taste, then mix this with the shallot and mushroom

mixture in the skillet. Heat this stuffing through gently.

5 Melt the remaining butter in a large saucepan. Squeeze the remaining lemon and add the juice to the pan with mushroom caps. Pour over just enough water to cover. Cook until the mushrooms are just tender. Drain them and fill with the stuffing. Arrange on a heated serving dish and serve hot.

Serves 4–8

Scallops Bonne Femme

16 large scallops, fresh or frozen
5½ cups button mushrooms
juice ½ lemon
3 shallots
1 cup heavy cream
1 cup dry white wine
salt and pepper
2 tablespoons butter

For the garnish:
sprigs of watercress
lemon wedges

1 Wash the scallops in cold water, dry them and cut the white flesh in half through the thickest section.

2 Trim the ends of the mushroom stalks. Wipe the mushrooms quickly, then slice them thinly. Pour the lemon juice over the mushrooms. Peel the shallots and mince them.

3 Put the mushrooms, shallots and scallop pieces into a saucepan. Add 3 tablespoons of the cream, the white wine and salt and pepper to taste. Cook over very high heat for about 10 minutes or until the liquid starts to turn syrupy.

4 Grease the scallop shells or a serving dish and heat it. Drain the scallop pieces, reserving the cooking liquid. Arrange them and the mushrooms in the hot scallop shells or in the serving dish.

5 Put the rest of the cream in the saucepan and beat with a whisk. Cut the butter into small pieces and add these to the cream all at once. Shake the saucepan to blend the sauce, check the seasoning, then pour over the scallops and mushrooms.

6 Garnish with sprigs of watercress and lemon wedges.

Serves 4

Scallops Bonne Femme — a tasty variation on the classic Coquilles St. Jacques

Stuffed Mushrooms with Shrimp Sauce

8 large mushrooms
2 cups small mushrooms
1 lemon
$\frac{1}{2}$ cup plus 2 tablespoons butter
salt and pepper
5 shallots
6 ozs. shelled shrimp
pinch paprika
2 tablespoons brandy
$\frac{1}{4}$ cup flour
$\frac{7}{8}$ cup milk
pinch cayenne pepper
$\frac{3}{4}$ cup heavy cream
1 tablespoon tomato catsup

1 Wash and dry the large and small mushrooms. Separate the stalks from the caps of the large mushrooms. Finely chop the stalks and the small mushrooms.

2 Squeeze the lemon. Put 2 tablespoons of the butter into a heavy-based saucepan, together with the lemon juice, and melt, stirring constantly. Add the large mushroom caps. Pour in just enough water to cover them. Season with salt and pepper and cook until the caps are just tender. Remove from the heat. Keep hot.

3 Peel and chop 2 of the shallots. Melt 2 tablespoons of the butter in a skillet. Add the shallots and finely chopped mushrooms and mix well. Add salt and pepper to taste and cook until all the liquid has evaporated. Remove from the heat. Keep hot.

4 Peel and chop the rest of the shallots. Melt 2 tablespoons of the butter in a small pan. Fry the shallots until they are golden-brown. Add half the shrimp and the paprika and cook, stirring, for 2 minutes. Sprinkle the brandy over the top and ignite it. When the flames die down, remove the pan from the heat. Keep hot.

5 Melt 2 tablespoons of the butter in a pan, draw off the heat and stir in the flour. Mix in half the milk, then add the rest. Return the pan to moderate heat and bring to boil,

stirring all the time. Simmer for 1-2 minutes and add a pinch of salt and cayenne pepper. Keep hot.

6 Put the remaining butter and shrimp, 1 tablespoon of the cream and salt and pepper to taste in a blender. Blend until smooth. Add to the chopped mushroom and shallot mixture and stir.

7 Add the shallot, shrimp and brandy mixture, the rest of the cream and the tomato catsup to the white sauce. Taste and adjust the seasoning.

8 Drain the 8 mushroom caps and place them, rounded sides down, on a heated serving plate. Fill them with the stuffing. Pour the sauce over the top and serve.

Tomato Quiche

For the pastry:
$2\frac{1}{4}$ cups flour
$\frac{1}{2}$ cup butter
pinch salt
3-4 tablespoons cold water

For the filling:
6-8 tomatoes
3 tablespoons olive oil
3 tablespoons tarragon and basil
pinch dried thyme
salt and freshly ground black pepper
1 tablespoon butter
4 eggs
$\frac{7}{8}$ cup light cream

1 Make the pastry by blending the flour and butter and adding the salt and water. Work together and when the pastry is smooth, roll it into a ball and let rest for an hour in the refrigerator.

2 Meanwhile, seed and chop the tomatoes. Heat the oil in a pan, add the tomatoes, tarragon, basil and

thyme and cook slowly. When they are cooked, pass them through a strainer and season well.

3 Preheat the oven to 400°F. Butter a deep quiche dish 8-9 inches in diameter. When the pastry has rested, roll it out and line the tin. Prick the bottom with a fork. Put it in the oven and cook for 10 minutes. Do not let the pastry brown.

4 Beat the eggs with the cream, salt and pepper. Add this to the tomato and herbs and mix. Pour the mixture into the quiche pan. Return to the oven at 375°F. and cook for 20-25 minutes. Serve hot or warm.

Serves 6–8

Artichokes with White Sauce

4 globe artichokes
$\frac{1}{2}$ lemon
4 tablespoons butter
5 tablespoons flour
$\frac{1}{2}$ cup light cream
salt and pepper

1 Carefully wash the artichokes. Break off the stem as near to the leaves as possible. Rub the bottoms with the half lemon.

2 Place the artichokes in a pan of salted water, bring to a boil and cook for 40 minutes. Drain, reserving the water.

3 Melt the butter in a saucepan. Add the flour and stir with a wooden spoon. Let cook for 3 minutes, making sure that the flour does not brown.

4 Add $1\frac{1}{4}$ cups of the artichoke water, while beating with a whisk. Bring to a boil whisking continually, then let cook on low heat for 10 minutes.

5 Fold the cream into the sauce. Allow it to boil for 2 minutes and then adjust the seasoning. Put the artichokes on a heated serving dish and serve the sauce from a sauceboat

Serves 4

Customer service: Box 1000, Brattleboro, VT 05301

Text typesetting in Times Roman and Souvenir
by A & B Typesetters, Inc., Concord   NH
Indexes in Helvetica by WordTech Corpor-
ation, Woburn   MA
Covers by Federated Lithographers,
Providence   RI
Printing and binding by Rand McNally,
Versailles   KY
Design and production by Unicorn Produc-
tion Services, Boston   MA
Publisher: Tom Begner
Editorial production: Kathy Shulga, Michael
Michaud
Staff: Erika Petersson, Pam Thompson

© Illustrations Bay Books Pty Ltd., Sydney,
Australia. Reprinted by permission.
© Illustrations from
"Les Cours de la Cuisine A à Z"
"Femmes d'Aujourd'hui"

ISBN 0-914575-01-5

For easy reference, the volumes are numbered
as follows:

1	1-96
2	97-192
3	193-288
4	289-384
5	385-480
6	481-576
7	577-672
8	673-768
9	769-864
10	865-960
11	961-1056
12	1057-1152